T0169040

A
Rose
By Many
Other Names

Rose Cherami and the JFK Assassination

Todd C. Elliott

Published by:
Trine Day LLC
PO Box 577
Walterville, OR 97489
1-800-556-2012
www.TrineDay.com
publisher@trineday.net

Library of Congress Control Number: 2013937965

Elliott, Todd C.
A Rose by Many Other Names: Rose Cherami and the JFK Assassination
—1st ed.
p. cm.

Epub (ISBN-13) 978-1-937584-64-1
Kindle (ISBN-13) 978-1-937584-65-8
Print (ISBN-13) 978-1-937584-63-4
1. Kennedy, John F. - (John Fitzgerald), - 1917-1963 - Assassination. 2. Cherami, Rose. I. Title

SECOND EDITION
10 9 8 7 6 5 4 3 2 1

Printed in the USA
Distribution to the Trade by:
Independent Publishers Group (IPG)
814 North Franklin Street
Chicago, Illinois 60610
312.337.0747
www.ipgbook.com

To the past, present and future people of Eunice, Louisiana.

Many thanks go out to the people of Mamou, Louisiana for helping me to accomplish my task.

And to the people would not and did not "go on the record" out of fear, may this book inspire you to share your knowledge of the truth.

con·spir·a·cy/ [kuhn-spir-uh-see] an evil, unlawful, treacherous, or surreptitious plan formulated in secret by two or more persons; plot.

She said she was going to, number one, pick up some money, pick up her baby, and to kill Kennedy.

– Lt. Francis Fruge, sworn testimony before the House Select Committee on Assassinations on Rose Cherami

White rose you are a stricken weary thing, shaming the spring . . .

– Hilda Doolittle

The committee believes, on the basis of the evidence available to it, that President John F. Kennedy was probably assassinated as a result of a conspiracy. The committee was unable to identify the other gunmen or the extent of the conspiracy.

– House Select Committee on Assassinations 95th Congress, March 1979

Foreword

The assassination of President John F. Kennedy on November 22, 1963 is one of the greatest tragedies in American history. In fact, the date 11/22/63 is synonymous with 12/7/41, "a date which will live in infamy" (to quote President Franklin Delano Roosevelt), the attack on Pearl Harbor, as well as 9/11/01, the terrorist attacks in New York, Washington, D.C. and Pennsylvania. Without question, the killing of JFK is America's greatest murder mystery, a case that has fascinated millions around the globe and spawned thousands of articles and hundreds of books. When studying this subject, it seems everyone is on a quest for the Holy Grail in this case- a definitive smoking gun.

This book contains one of those elusive smoking guns.

A Rose By Many Other Names: Rose Cherami and the JFK Assassination by Todd C. Elliott is a very worthwhile book- do not let the relatively small size fool you, as good things do indeed often come in small packages. This is an all-in-one-place volume that dissects the saga of Rose Cherami, whose remarkable clairvoyance regarding the impending assassination is a mighty compelling story, to put it mildly. Cherami's story was briefly depicted at the very start of Oliver Stone's hit movie JFK, as well as in a few other works on the subject, yet no one had ever put together the definitive source on this compelling woman.

Until now, that is.

Elliott is to be commended for an impressive to-the-point writing style and compiling a nice selection of photos, as well. Along with the Secret Service agents of mysterious repute on the grassy knoll and the Joseph Milteer prediction, the Rose Cherami story is a smoking gun in the Kennedy case that goes far beyond clinical arguments about ballistics, magic bullets and eyewitness testimony. In short, it is an important touchstone (or Rosetta Stone) into unlocking the keys to the ultimate solution to this case. There is no other way to put it: the Cherami story demonstrates the impending conspiracy to take the life of our 35th president.

Kudos to Todd Elliott for masterfully telling her story. She would be proud.

Vince Palamara
Author of *Survivor's Guilt, JFK: From Parkland to Bethesda,* and *The Not So Secret Service*
Pittsburgh, PA
August 15, 2016

Notes From the Past

Sometimes in the America, the truth comes too late. But sometimes the truth comes too early.

Such is the strange case and tale of Rose Cherami. This story, in itself, does not only take an unflinching look at the life of the woman who "forecasted" the imminent assassination of the 35th President of the United States, John F. Kennedy, but also at the Louisiana connections to the murder of the president.

Rose was merely one of the many Louisiana connections to the JFK assassination. There are more plumes of smoke emitting from Louisiana in the fire that was the JFK assassination and investigation. There are, without a doubt, more Louisiana ties to the murder of JFK than Texas.

Take, for example, the alleged shooter, Lee Harvey Oswald of New Orleans. Oswald was a native son of Louisiana and the supposed killer of President Kennedy. However, Oswald appeared to have made a name for himself in New Orleans during the summer of 1963 on radio and television as a vehement Marxist-Leninist member of the Communist Party, according to his words. Oswald was born in New Orleans and grew up some 22 miles north of New Orleans in Covington, Louisiana in an area commonly referred to as "The Northshore" of the New Orleans Metropolitan area. It is the Northshore area of LaCombe, Louisiana – where Cuban exiles were trained for the Bay of Pigs invasion of Cuba to overthrow Fidel Castro at the start of the turbulent sixties.

Jim Garrison, the Orleans Parish District Attorney and the first and only man to bring a trial in the murder of President

Kennedy. His case began with news reports of Oswald, paraded on national television as the lone assassin of the President, who spent time in New Orleans as a rabid communist. Garrison's case began with a single step into the investigation of Oswald in 1963 and culminated in 1967 with an official and widely publicized investigative murder case.

Clay LaVerne Shaw, of Kentwood, Louisiana, was the director of the International Trade Mart in New Orleans at the time of the JFK assassination. Shaw was the man that Garrison brought to trial, charging him with being part of a conspiracy to assassinate President Kennedy. Shaw was the first and only person brought to trial for the murder of the President.

Congressman Thomas Hale Boggs, a member of the U.S. House of Representatives who represented Louisiana's 2nd Congressional district, was chosen to be a member of the President's Commission on the Assassination of President Kennedy (or the Warren Commission), to help investigate the murder of President Kennedy. It is said that Congressman Boggs might have possibly relayed information to Garrison and that the U.S. Senator Russell Long (of the Louisiana Long family dynasty) character in the "JFK" Oliver Stone film (portrayed by Walter Matthau) was based on Boggs' role in the sequence of actual events. Boggs appeared to have a "dissenting opinion," according to some, of the investigation by the Warren Commission into the assassination of President Kennedy. Boggs was allegedly one who questioned the veracity and amount of hard evidence submitted to the Warren Commission by the FBI and CIA. Boggs was also credited with believing that the U.S. intelligence agencies withheld information and evidence in the assassination of the president. Boggs even questioned the former head of the CIA, Allen Dulles, into a confirmation that the CIA had a track record of employing people like Oswald for intelligence and counter-intelligence service. Publicly, Boggs was also very critical of J. Edgar Hoover, the Director of the FBI at the time, more critical than most or any of the Warren Commission members. The Louisiana Representative

Hale Boggs subsequently went missing on October 16, 1972 during a campaign flight from Anchorage, Alaska to Juneau, Alaska. The plane carrying Boggs is believed to have crashed as the Congressman is believed to have been killed in the plane crash. However, the body of the Congressman from Louisiana and serving member of The Warren Commission has never been found to this day.

Another Louisiana figure is Carlos Marcello, born Calogero Minacori in Africa. Marcello was considered by some as "the Godfather of Louisiana." Marcello was a Italian mafioso who, it is believed, had motive to kill the President John F. Kennedy. Before that, he became head of the Louisiana organized crime families in the 1940s and reigned for more than 30 years. His name still strikes fear in the hearts and souls in Louisiana today.

And then there was Rose. She was a Texas girl who had become a lower-level operative, a "mule" in the world of organized crime with drug and sex trafficking possibly as far back as the late 1940s. She was the woman who showed up, or didn't show up, in the pages of American history on November 20, 1963.

She never seemed to stop running all over the country, as the following chapters will reveal. She ran so much in fact, before and after the assassination of JFK that one could only wonder if her alias "Rose Cherami" could be an anagram for "Mi Racehorse," which could translate easily in Italian or Spanish as "My Racehorse."

The author would prefer it duly noted that the first edition of this work was published in August of 2013, months before the 50th anniversary of the JFK assassination. While there is no documentation to prove the author's claim and Amazon.com will list the book publication date as September 19, 2013, the truth, once again, came ahead of schedule. The truth, it seems, doesn't have a schedule or a deadline.

Even after the submitted manuscript went to press, the books were printer and the boxes were shipped, the truth continued to bombard the author with more information about Rose Cherami and other characters and places that will be explored in the following chapters.

Starting with the beginning of Rose's life in Texas, where she was born Melba Christine Youngblood, not Melba Christine Marcades.

Rose was not born in Houston, but rather in Dallas, according to birth certificate records allegedly obtained by Rose Cherami's son, Michael Marcades.

According to Rose's Louisiana State Penitentiary transfer sheet dated November 9, 1942, Dallas is listed as her place of birth while her home address is listed as 4114 Dallas Street, Houston, Texas. In fact, many times according to her arrest records both Houston and Dallas are listed as her city of birth.

It is believed by Marcades family members that Rose was born at home and not in a hospital. Furthermore, her family moved to Houston – where her father Thomas Youngblood worked as a farmer – shortly after her birth. The alleged only surviving member of Rose's immediate family is Michael Marcades, who appears in one of the final chapters of this work. And during the time of the 50th anniversary of the JFK assassination commemoration in Dallas, Michael was scheduled to appear at a small speaking engagement before a gathering of JFK researchers and enthusiasts from all over the world. However, Michael Marcades was now being billed as "Michael Cherami" in a family tradition perhaps that began with his mother and her long list of aliases. More than likely, it was a scheduling error on the event planner's part and it was unknown as to whether or not Michael chose to be billed as "Michael Cherami."

It should be noted that during the author's initial (and only) meeting with the son of Rose Cherami, Michael Marcades held back a lot of the truth and answers to the mysteries of his mother. Much to this author's chagrin, Marcades chose to arrive to the interview with his own publisher and refused to answer many of the author's questions, based on the advice of his would-be publisher. Michael, apparently, wanted to save some things for his own version, which has been delayed for some time and still, to the best of my knowledge at the time, is not yet available in print. Michael did, however, let it be known that the first edition of this book was inaccurate when stating that his mother was born in Houston. She was born, according to Michael's Facebook avatar, in Dallas. Yet, while there was a birth certificate, the author of this work was not granted access to the document to verify his claim.

No matter, for to the author and most of the JFK researchers and truth seekers in the world, the woman we know as Rose Cherami was born in U.S. history on November 20, 1963 in Eunice, Louisiana. For more than 50 years, the world knew very little more than that about Rose.

Also after submitting the final draft of this work for printing, the author noticed that in the transcripts of Air Force One in Dallas on November 22, 1963, the name "Youngblood" came up again in the JFK Assassination. One chapter of this book is entitled "Young Blood." This chapter investigates the Youngblood name and the coincidences and appearances of this surname in the investigation of the assassination of JFK.

A Secret Service Agent, Rufus Youngblood, was in Dealey Plaza the day that Kennedy was killed. Rufus Youngblood, code named "Dagger," was given the duty of protecting Vice-President Lyndon B. Johnson in his limousine during the fateful motorcade on November 22, 1963. Rufus Youngblood was also in charge of the Johnson family's safety following the assassination of JFK. Rufus Youngblood also drew the criticism and ire of some JFK researchers, who claimed that Rufus Youngblood dove in front of LBJ in a motion of protective cover before, or nearly before, the shots were heard in Dealey Plaza. To some researchers, Rufus Youngblood's possibly premature motioning and movements indicated that he might have anticipated the Dallas shootings in Dealey Plaza. Some might even suggest that Youngblood was possibly involved in the planning or the plotting of the assassination. Following the assassination of Kennedy and the Kennedy administration, Rufus Youngblood was granted a promotion under the Johnson administration to become the new head of the Secret Service.

The author toyed with the idea that a person of interest, who was mentioned in the "Young Blood" chapter, might possibly be Rufus Youngblood.

If so, "Jack Youngblood" or "Johnny Youngblood," who caught the attention of Garrison investigators in regards to Rose and her source of foreknowledge, did it pose another set of questions?

Could Rose have been a relative to Jack Youngblood, a known criminal and possible assassin?

Could Rose have been related by blood to Rufus Youngblood, who now worked as a Secret Service agent?

So many questions need answers even when there are very little. The author compared dates of a Jack Youngblood, of Georgia, and his criminal record never overlaps and seemingly synchronize with the upstart Secret Service career of Rufus Youngblood, also of Georgia. As the trail on the Atlanta, Georgia-based criminal, "Jack Youngblood" ends in 1951, the rise of "Rufus Youngblood" of the Atlanta field office of the United States Secret Service begins. Both of the "Youngblood" men appeared to have a military record and experience as a pilot or service in the aviation field. Rufus was a former United States Army Air Corps veteran of World War II.

What if Rufus Youngblood and Jack Youngblood were the same person?

If so, then that would mean that the United States Secret Service would have to be complicit in hiring a veteran with a known criminal record following WWII and securing a new identity for the recruit. There is no evidence to prove that Secret Service agents could be given a new name for the protection of their own identity.

Even if they are not the same man, could either one be related to Melba Christine Youngblood, the given birth name of Rose Cherami?

Rose would not necessarily have to be linked to the state of Georgia in some way. While there is no proof of Rose in Atlanta or Georgia, it should be noted that one of the last aliases used by Rose was one with a last name of "Clinkscales." The interesting thing about that Scottish surname is that it can be found in several states in the continental United States, predominantly, in Georgia and South Carolina.

Clint Hill, who was the first Secret Service to reach the back of the Kennedy's limousine in Dealey Plaza following the fatal shots, along with Youngblood were regarded as national heroes following the assassination of President Kennedy.

Hill was bestowed an award from the US Secretary of the Treasury Clarence Douglas Dillon, while Rufus would receive his commendation from the new commander in chief. Hill was the first of the two agents to be awarded the US Treasury Gold Medal, according to a now-vintage Universal-International News newsreel.

The next day, the newly-made President Lyndon B. Johnson (who did not attend the Clint Hill ceremony) decided to cite the Secret Service agent assigned to him. Curiously, Rufus Youngblood was presented with the US Treasury Gold Medal by President Johnson in the White House rose garden.

Though Hill would go on to receive more acclaim, Rufus Youngblood went on to have a promotion and a furthered career in Secret Service. However, Youngblood's career was cut short during the Nixon administration.

The commemoration was forever preserved in a historic Universal-International News newsreel in which LBJ gave a speech about Rufus Youngblood saying, "There is no more heroic act than offering your life to save another. And in that awful moment of confusion, when all about him were losing their heads, Rufus Youngblood never lost his."

Less than two weeks after the assassination of JFK, LBJ used those poorly chosen and tasteless words on December 4, 1963. Words, which are chosen by the president's speech writer or himself, often leave nothing to chance or scrutiny.

Through LBJ we learn that Rufus never lost his head. The implied and never spoken fact is that Kennedy did lose his head. Kennedy's name was also notably absent from of LBJ's sound bite and from the audio commentary of the newsreel announcer.

Following the published first edition of this work, it should be noted that when LBJ's aforementioned, poorly chosen words were paraphrased by the author during a lecture at Loyola University in New Orleans, the audience let out a collective gasp of horror. As in the case of the author, the affect of LBJ's words were apparently received differently, albeit to a different audience, nearly 50 years later.

Before President Kennedy met his untimely death, Eunice, Louisiana was where folks first heard Rose's truth about the assassination of President John F. Kennedy on the Wednesday before that fateful Friday in Dallas. And following the 50th year commemoration of the Kennedy assassination, people in Eunice and people in Dallas were still hearing talk about Rose in Eunice.

The author thought that it should be noted here that upon the release of the first edition of this book, the people of Eunice seemed to be deeply affected by this book. While some declared to the author that they read the book two and three times, others declared that the book jogged their memories.

A perhaps blocked out memory, was now loose again within the community and people were talking about it and remembering and sharing memories, thoughts and ideas. The bobcat was out of the bag, it seemed, in Eunice as a dirty secret had been aired and people could finally talk about it without fear of repercussions.

Mrs. Jane Carrier, the widow of L.G. Carrier, who witnessed Rose at Moosa Hospital in Eunice and heard her say the things that she said, told the author what she could remember as it seemed to come back to her after publication. It came as a more detailed account of her husband's story.

Mrs. Carrier said that two different individuals, over a span of 25 years to 30 years on two separate occasions, came to the Carrier home seeking information about Rose. Carrier, obviously, was a person of interest. He must have been someone to talk to about a woman named Rose and that whole JFK thing.

One man – who came as recently as 2001 – claimed that he paid a visit to L.G. Carrier to interview him on behalf of Rose's son, Michael, whom he claimed was aiding in gathering research on his mother for a book. This man with the last name of "Tobin" or "Toblin" claimed that he was from Texas.

Mrs. Jane Carrier said that he was certainly pleasant enough, drinking coffee with her and L.G. and chatting in the kitchen of their Eunice home.

However, this "Tobin" appeared on the Carrier's door step more than once. And prior his last visit and requested interview, Mr. Carrier had become gravely ill and could not visit or give another interview to this Mr. Tobin. Mr. Tobin still persisted as Mrs. Carrier did most of the talking after that. L.G. wasn't feeling up to it anymore due to his illness, according to Mrs. Carrier. Mr. Carrier soon succumbed to his illness shortly after.

But no interview of L.G. Carrier has ever been published. Nor had Michael Marcades hired anyone to do any research on his mother, according to Michael himself.

Another man then appeared on the doorstep of the Carrier house sometime around 1976. Clearly he identified himself, even though Mrs. Carrier could not remember who this mystery man was. She did recall, however, that he sat down on the couch in their living room and just simply listened to what Mr. Carrier had to say about Rose Cherami and the strange events that led up to the murder of the President of The United States.

Mrs. Carrier said that the "mystery man" did not take out one pen or pencil, did not write down one note on a pad of paper, nor did he take any audio recordings of the conversation that he and Mr. Carrier had one day. After hearing everything that Mr. Carrier could remember, the man simply got up from the couch, said his formal good-bye and walked out their front door into obscurity.

According to Mrs. Carrier, about six or seven months later, her husband received a letter from the Federal Bureau of Investigations. Mr. Carrier was selected as a member of law enforcement to be a candidate for the FBI training academy. He opted not to go to the FBI training academy.

Again, it should be pointed out that the "mystery man" interview with L.G. Carrier marked two interviews that have yet to be published.

It was then that Mrs. Carrier shared another memory about L.G. Carrier and Rose Cherami. Being a police officer, he was present at the old Eunice city jail when Rose Cherami was brought in on November 20, 1963.

According to Jane Carrier, L.G. confided in her that he would never forget the screaming, shouting and animal-like sounds that Rose emitted as they forced her into a holding cell. L.G. told his wife that it took two men to put her behind bars as she was flailing, kicking and dragging her heels.

According to Jane Carrier, her husband L.G. said that at one point Rose was just shouting out names, names of people. The author noted that it would have been interesting to hear some of those names that Rose was shouting in her state. Due to lack of documentation, one can only imagine that the names that Rose frantically spoke may have even had a familiar ring to JFK researchers some 50 years later.

But Mrs. Carrier said that, at the time, L.G. Carrier didn't really pay attention to the names that Rose shouted in the Eunice city jail. After all, everyone thought that Rose was crazy and/or on drugs.

The coroner was soon called in. And doctors would play a significant role Rose's life.

There's the interesting statement of Mr. A.H. Magruder, who described himself as a 47 year-old self-employed manufacture representative, made a statement about Rose's story and how it involved a psychiatrist that worked at the East Louisiana State Hospital in Jackson, Louisiana, not far from where Magruder lived in St. Francisville.

According to a memo by District Attorney Jim Garrison, dated February 23, 1967, Magruder claimed that Dr. Victor J. Weiss related a story to him during the Christmas holidays of 1963. Magruder claimed that Dr. Weiss said prior to the Kennedy assassination, Louisiana State Police picked up a woman on Highway 190 near Eunice, Louisiana.

After the State Police brought Rose to the East Louisiana State Hospital in Jackson, the memo concludes:

"Dr. Weiss gave her a thorough physical and psychiatric examination and determined that she was a narcotic addict and was having withdrawal symptoms. She told him that she worked as a dope runner for Jack Ruby. I believe she also mentioned that she worked in the night club for Ruby and that she was forced to go to Florida with another man whom she did not name to pick up a shipment of dope to take back to Dallas, that she didn't want to do this thing but she had a young child and that they would hurt her child if she didn't."

"She also told Dr. Weiss that the President and other Texas Public Officials were going to be killed on their visit to Dallas. Dr. Weiss said that he really didn't pay much attention to a woman of this type until after the assassination occurred at which time he went back to this woman who was still in the hospital and had further conversation with her."

According to the memo, Rose claimed to have seen Oswald sitting at the same table with Ruby at one of Ruby's clubs but did not elaborate any further.

Contrary to testimony that the Louisiana State Police were dispatched to the state hospital to retrieve Rose, Magruder claimed that the FBI came to East Louisiana State Hospital and picked this woman up. He also claimed that Dr. Weiss had to sign the papers for her release at the time.

Hand-written notes alongside a copy of the memo, indicate that Garrison's team were hearing a different version of the

Jackson hospital story in that the FBI arrived to pick up Rose. Even though Magruder's recollection may be mistaken about the FBI coming to get Rose on Monday, it detracts from Lt. Francis Fruge's sworn testimony. It is possible, however, that the FBI did pay a visit to the East Louisiana State Hospital in Jackson, Louisiana at some point in regards to Rose.

Another curious clue in Garrison's Rose Cherami file is a handwritten letter by an unsigned author. The letter dated July 29, 1967 – read:

"Notes on a case in Charity hospital, New Orleans, Louisiana. On July 4th I met a young woman from a small town in East Texas who told me this tale. She heard it from a doctor in Shreveport who also practices in New Orleans. On November 22, 1963 early in the morning a woman brought into Charity Hospital was in a deplorable state, suffering from exposure, beating, etc. She was unconscious, probably under narcotics. Later in the day she revived and the intern told her that John F. Kennedy had been assassinated in Dallas and a fellow named Oswald had been picked up and charged with the killing. Her reaction was 'Did they get Ruby too?' No one thought much of it until Sunday when Ruby shot Oswald. The woman had been discharged by then and when the FBI was told of this they could not find a trace of her. So much for that!"

Rose was many things to many different people. She was also a French Quarter dweller.

There was, in fact, another doctor in Rose's life in The French Quarter.

On the edge of the French Quarter, in the 1000 block of Esplanade Avenue, in a palatial Victorian home lived a Dr. Warren J. Stassi. His address, 1004 Esplanade, was Rose's address. It was one of the final addresses listed by Rose during her final arrest.

How, after the assassination of JFK, could this woman, Rose Cherami, live in such a palatial home? Was she merely renting a room as a lodger?

The author speculated that a doctor could have been one to facilitate Rose's drug problem and addiction. A doctor could have also earned enough money to afford to pay Rose to keep quiet. There is also the possibility that, given the location of the house in the French Quarter during the 1960s, the house could have been a whorehouse. It was believed, according to property records, that Dr. Stassi and his wife lived at the address. However, Mr. and Mrs. Stassi could have been merely property owners at the time and not residents of the property.

It should also be noted that around the corner from 1004 Esplanade, less than two blocks away, was 1313 Dauphine Street. This infamous address was one of the many properties of and (at the time)the home of Clay Shaw. Rose and Shaw must have been neighbors in the geographical sense of the term for a time shortly after the Kennedy assassination. It's possible that they knew one another. It's possible that they were neighbors before JFK was assassinated. What seems impossible is that two significant Louisiana figures and key footnotes in the JFK assassination lived within walking distance of one another.

After the author of this work published a photograph of the house and the researched history of the property on the Facebook page for this book, members of the Marcades family came forward and were interested in this factoid about Rose and Dr. Stassi of New Orleans.

According to Marcades family members, Dr. Stassi was an ear, nose and throat doctor who worked at Charity Hospital in New Orleans. Rose's stated occupation at the time of the address was that of a "Bar Maid" from Cut Off, Louisiana, according to her October 21, 1964 arrest record from the New Orleans Police Department. The origin of the surname "Cherami" was native to only one region in Louisiana: Cut Off, Louisiana and the surrounding area.

Another strange piece of circumstantial evidence in the Garrison research files on Rose came in the form of a job application of another doctor, one whose life could have possibly tied into Rose's life. Within Garrison's investigative files on Rose are Louisiana state job applications for at least two physicians and their relationship with the East Louisiana State Hospital in Jackson, Louisiana.

The first doctor that caught Garrison's investigative eye was Malcom Gray Pierson, who applied for a "Physician II" position with the State of Louisiana Department of Civil Service. According to his application, Dr. Pierson did not desire to work anywhere else in the state in February of 1964, other than the East Louisiana State Hospital in Jackson. Living at 655 Polytech Drive in Baton Rouge, Louisiana, Dr. Pierson also stated that he desired to take the physician examination in Jackson, Louisiana. It should be noted that Garrison's investigators circled this answer on his application.

This comes across as curious at first glance; the fact that a doctor, who lived in the state capital, apply for a State of Louisiana Department of Civil Service job and offer to drive nearly an hour when it could be done in Baton Rouge. However, Dr. Pierson's application reflected that he was currently employed at the Jackson facility as a Physician I and was merely doing the proper paperwork in applying for the Physician II position.

Born in 1924, the 40 year-old Dr. Pierson would have been about the same age as Rose. And it also seemed that he shared some of her bad habits. His application listed a 1962 "narcotic violation" complete with what appears on the application as a five-year suspension. He appeared to complete his apparent narcotic "treatment" in 1963. Dr. Pierson listed on his application that he was given a full pardon in 1964.

Dr. Pierson had worked at the East Louisiana State Hospital in Jackson since August of 1963. His application listed that he worked in the white female infirmary ward at the state mental hospital. So this means that, even following his narcotics violation in 1962, Dr. Pierson was allowed to work at the Jackson hospital and was possibly present when Rose was admitted on November 21, 1963. His interest in narcotics could also validate a possibility that he knew Rose outside of the hospital as well.

Dr. Pierson even listed his military career which denoted that he had service in a branch of the US military during wartime with honorable or satisfactory discharge from 1943 to 1946 and 1951 to 1953 and from 1956 to 1958 in the United States Naval Reserve under serial number 541225. In 1956, according to his application, Dr. Pierson was also employed full-time at the US Navy Personnel Department in Washington, D.C.

Pierson's application listed three character references. One was a doctor whose name popped up from time to time in the investigation of Rose Cherami, Dr. Frank Silva of the East Louisiana State Hospital. Had Pierson been hired for the position he would have been in a position to have access to Rose's patient records and files, before and after the assassination of President John F. Kennedy.

The second Louisiana State Department of Civil Service application that caught the attention of Garrison's team was a younger doctor, Dr. Joseph Augustine Rozas, from Alexandria, Louisiana. Aside from his character references being from Charity Hospital in New Orleans, Dr. Rozas' March 1961 application was not as suspect as Dr. Pierson's. However, Dr. Rozas had a Metairie address that was nearly identical to one that Rose Cherami gave during her final days. Rozas listed on his job application an address of 704 Orion Street in Metairie, Louisiana. Rose had listed in 1964 an address of 757 Orion Street in Metairie.

Whether it was just another of the many string of coincidences in the multitude of JFK research, what is known is that Rose was living within the same house and city blocks of doctors. Whatever lifestyle she had, it was one that brought her into some of the same neighborhoods and even homes of known doctors in the New Orleans area.

Was there a "medical angle" to the JFK Assassination and the significant cover-up that followed? If so, why?

If author of *Me & Lee*, Judyth Vary Baker, and author of *Dr. Mary's Monkey*, Edward T. Haslam, are to be believed, this link between Rose and New Orleans area doctors could be another small piece in a huge puzzle.

The pieces didn't always fit and witnesses didn't always talk. Many, out of fear for their own safety refused to go "on the record" with the author of this work.

One of those who refused to go "on the record" about Rose was Mrs. Anne Dischler, of Eunice, Louisiana. Dischler was one of the first people that the author of this work interviewed regarding Rose. By late January 2014, Dischler decided to go on the record about Rose and the anti-hero of this work, Lt. Francis Fruge of the Louisiana State Police. As Fruge was one of the only people to give sworn testimony before the HSCA in the late 1970s, Dischler alluded to the fact that Fruge knew more than he let on during the 1970s investigations. In fact, Dischler said that she believed that Fruge did not just happen to meet Rose on November 20, 1963 at the Moosa Hospital in Eunice. She said that the staff called Fruge into the hospital because of the fact that he was very familiar with Rose and whom she worked for.

By 1967, Dischler was working with Fruge as an undercover agent and assistant investigator in the field on various cases. Dischler often wore a wig and donned an alias in effort to portray a "B-Girl." But when the 1967 investigation of Garrison opened up, a lawyer-investigator by the name of Frank Meloche was dispatched to Crowley, Louisiana, whence Dischler and Fruge embarked upon a trip to Houston and then flew to Dallas.

"We went to Dallas to see where JFK was killed," said Dischler. "We had three or four, maybe as many as five Dallas policemen with us in Dealey Plaza. And they showed us everything and where it all happened. They showed us where they said that a gunmen stood behind a fence on the grassy knoll area. But none of them would go on the record or testify. They said that there was also four or five marksmen, one up on the overpass and one would shoot. Also they told us that one was on the overpass, one on the grassy knoll, one in the book depository and one in the storm drain. They weren't going to let Kennedy get away. They told us everything by mouth, but you couldn't get anybody to give you a statement."

Dischler stated that Fruge knew Rose and knew how to get in contact with her parents, who were living in the Dallas-Fort Worth area at the time.

"Francis knew that I had an alias and that I could use it so that I could effectively lie about who I was," said Dischler. "My heart went out to poor Rose, but she chose that life. Fruge said for me to call Rose's mother, Minnie Stroud, and I called and pretended to be Rose's friend. And she received that and she talked to me. She told me Rose was dead. She talked to me pretty easily. But I didn't stay on the phone very long with her. Francis knew how to get a hold of her mom because he knew where Rose was from originally. And when they said that she was killed up there on the highway near Big Sandy, Francis knew where she was and he's the one that told Frank Meloche that he knew her well when we first got in the car to go to Dallas."

After arriving in Dallas, Dischler made her phone call to Rose's parents from a hotel room. She was convinced that Rose and Fruge had been familiar with one another for years before November 20, 1963.

"Fruge had gotten her out of more than one crack," said Dischler. "Francis knew her ... and she covered territory all over the southern part of Louisiana, for sure, and into Texas. And from town to town ... she'd always stay in touch with Francis and his higher-ups, mainly Captain Ben Morgan. They did not want her in Louisiana anymore. Francis, if he didn't know exactly where she was, he would hear from her. She reported in and would have to do that. She reported in to the state officials who were protecting her."

If Dischler is to be believed, some Louisiana State Police officials could be seen as complicit in the efforts of drug trafficking in the state. Perhaps many of Rose's arrests and drug busts were merely procedure for drug seizures, pay-offs or gaining information from Rose about upcoming drug traffic, and deliveries. Dischler claimed that Rose knew Louisiana State Police Captain Ben Morgan "very well."

Only one person in Louisiana law enforcement testified about Rose, even though the names of Captain Ben Morgan and Trooper Wayne Morein are often mentioned in the tale of Rose. These were two other credible witnesses to Rose and her claims. Fruge, it seemed, was the sole spokesperson for the strange case of Rose Cherami. It was Fruge who testified about the incident at The Silver Slipper whorehouse in Evangeline Parish, on the outskirts of Eunice.

Dischler, who was also mentioned in the published HSCA report, said that Fruge's testimony in 1978 was selective. When asked if it was credible, Dischler said that "most of it" was credible.

"There was only portions that the HSCA wanted to ask," said Dischler. "Rose was so widespread in Texas, Louisiana and Mississippi also."

It should be noted that the author of this work, who traveled through Mississippi to interview Rose's son, took note of a roadside RV campground in Mississippi named "The Silver Slipper," which is matching in name to The Silver Slipper Casino operating to this day outside of Bay St. Louis. Coupled with another bar and music venue named The Silver Slipper in Leonville, Louisiana that still operated as of 2013, this would have been yet one of many places known as "The Silver Slipper" on Rose's route through the Gulf Coast.

Dischler said that Fruge was familiar with Jack Ruby, as Ruby was one with a notorious reputation. She also stated that it was possible that Ruby would often stop in Eunice on his way to New Orleans, which was another claim made by another individual following the publication of the first edition of this work. Russ Bordelon, of Lake Charles, stated in an email that it was well-known that Ruby would stay in a motel on Highway 190 called La Parisienne (The motel still exists in modern Eunice as the "Eunice Inn").

It should be noted that two anonymous sources, one prior to the first edition of this book and one after the first edition of this book, claimed that Lee Harvey Oswald was also rumored to have been seen in Eunice. One man claimed that a local shop owner, who had a storefront on Highway 190, was approached by a man, who was later unofficially identified as Oswald. This "Oswald" offered to wash the store windows in an effort to earn money to travel to Dallas.

Another Oswald tale, told for years among locals, is one that involved Oswald's connection to the regional crime element of Eunice and Mamou. It is believed that the Marcello-connected mobsters of the region were tasked with entertaining Oswald, who stopped on his way to Dallas. It is said that the Cajun crime lords offered to get Oswald laid at one of the many whorehouses in Eunice and Mamou, before he left for Dallas.

If these claims are true, could Rose have encountered Oswald prior to the assassination?

To discredit that local legend is one thing. To explore it is another.

The story that has persisted for decades in Eunice is a story that could have been misinterpreted by locals over the years. It's possible that when the story originated, it was one that told of "JFK's assassin," not Oswald, who was shown a good time while in Cajun Country. Perhaps the story had possibly shifted and changed to a story about Oswald, who was now dead and considered by the Warren Commission to be the lone assassin of President Kennedy. Using the name Oswald after he was dead was probably a "safe name" to use. The name Oswald, which was one that everyone knew, was a safe bet when retelling tales rather than naming the names of the actual mysterious shooters, or shooter, that allegedly traveled through Eunice with Rose in tow on November 20, 1963. Whatever the story may be, it belongs to Rose Cherami in its origin and is one that deserves further examination.

Table of Contents

Foreword by Vince Palamara ix

Preface to Second Edition: Notes from the Past xi

One – A Rose By Many Other Names 1

Two – The Legend Arose 7

Three – The Register 13

Four – Meanwhile Back at the Eunice Jail 19

Five – Going to Jackson 23

Six – Good Doctor, Bad Doctor 29

Seven – Little Big Mamou 33

Eight – Her Life and Her Life of Crime 41

Nine – Young Blood 53

Ten – The Long D.O.A. of Rose Cherami 61

Eleven – Son of Rose Cherami 67

Epilogue – First Person, Last Words 73

Index 81

The woman who would be known as Rose Cherami, circa 1946.
""Dead ends were the plan – by those who saw to it that her life was cut short."
Courtesy of Dr. Michael Marcades

Chapter One

A Rose By Many Other Names

While the credits roll at the beginning of Oliver Stone's 1991 film *JFK*, there is a glimpse of Rose Cherami. In between the edited, historic film footage, Rose Cherami is immortalized in the first dramatized sequence of the film, as the stunt double for actress Sally Kirkland is thrown from a moving vehicle. In the dust, a screaming and crying woman is on the side of a rural highway cursing at the car speeding away ahead of her.

The film then cuts to the woman, hysterical in a hospital bed, telling law enforcement and medical staff that "they're going to Dallas ... Friday ... they're going to kill Kennedy." The characters in the film, much as in life, paid her no mind.

This was Rose Cherami. She predicted the future. She did it in a small Louisiana town named Eunice.

Eunice as the birthplace of JFK assassination theory has more credence than the widely accepted "magic bullet theory," simply because the first public revelation of a plot to kill the 35th President of the United States resounded from the lips of one Melba Marcades, also known as Rose Cherami, in that small town.

Ruling out conspiracy, then certainly the woman was clairvoyant. Ruling out clairvoyance, one must talk of foreknowledge, and then again back to conspiracy. A tip from Rose, two days before the assassination, would forever link the city of Eunice to the JFK assassination plot.

Some people of Eunice, mainly members of law enforcement and medical officials, were the first to hear talk of a conspiracy involving shooters in Dallas, two days before

John Fitzgerald Kennedy was assassinated in what is still, legally and officially, an unsolved crime for the Dallas Police Department.

Eunice is home to folks of the Cajun Prairie. They are a friendly people who know that Eunice is a small town, and they seemingly strive to keep it that way, content with its charm, size and the rate of growth. It is a unique Louisiana town of the best Cajun people, food and music in the world.

During World War II, "Camp Eunice" was established by the United States Army as a prisoner-of-war camp, holding German and Italian POWs who were made to work in the rice fields south of town.

Today most of the Eunice residents know the area of POW Camp Eunice as the Tri-Parish Fairgrounds. An abandoned Louisiana Army National Guard Armory rests near the corner of the former POW camp grounds, which are now buried like a secret under weathered tennis courts and baseball fields contained within a surrounding neighborhood.

A day in Eunice in 2013 was much as it would have been in 1963. Even an element of vice remained in the culture as it was in 1963.

Those who remember 1963 can recall slot machines in the local grocery stores – where if a shopper chanced to have some spare change they might then press their luck and have a little gamble on the "one-armed bandits." Those in the know back then could guess at the source of the slot machines and the vice: New Orleans and some of the organized crime therein.

A vibrant nightlife – with places like the Purple Peacock, the Oleander and the Silver Slipper along the highway – made a neon offering of live music, wild women and an escape from the small-town doldrums. Back-room card games were the norm, invisibly framed by one-way mirrors in case of a raid or someone forgetting to pay off the local sheriff.

Such was life along U.S. Highway 190, or the "Acadiana Trail," in 1963.

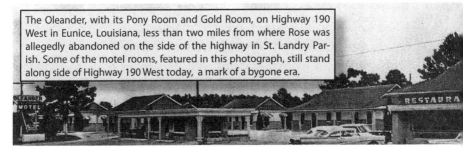

The Oleander, with its Pony Room and Gold Room, on Highway 190 West in Eunice, Louisiana, less than two miles from where Rose was allegedly abandoned on the side of the highway in St. Landry Parish. Some of the motel rooms, featured in this photograph, still stand along side of Highway 190 West today, a mark of a bygone era.

If Orleans Parish District Attorney, Jim Garrison, was *On The Trail of the Assassins*, as his book title suggested, it's quite possible that the Acadiana Trail was the very trail that led to the murder of JFK in Dallas.

Today, the video poker machines are relegated to their own domains in the form of truckstop casinos or the small, off-chance casinos open day and night in modern Eunice. Today, however, when the house wins, the government for the state of Louisiana also wins.

At the end of any day, wherever a resident or visitor might decide to lay their head for the night in Eunice, the chugging, horn blast of a train or the ringing of a church bell is always within earshot. The streets of Eunice near the quaint town square are windswept with rice hulls in the late Summer under the watchful gaze of a towering, rusted rice mill that has seen better days.

The old aluminum buildings that are the rice mill and rice dryer stand as the tallest structures in the city. At nearly four stories high, like some "cajun skyscrapers," they seemingly oversee all business and living transacted in Eunice. All others are height relegated to not exceed two stories.

Before Interstate 10 – connecting Houston with New Orleans to the south – siphoned off the traffic and much of the commerce to Eunice, U.S. Highway 190 was the 1963 equivalent. With the advent of I-10, Eunice remained much as it was then, with only sparse and sporadic growth over the decades.

It was here where a momentous fragment of American history was born. And as with all birthing processes, there is an element of pain before delivery. Even a legend must cling to something before it breathes to life and manifests out of the ether. However, a legend would insinuate a myth.

But it is not by any mythos, but by way of history, that Eunice has been linked to the crime of the 20th century: the murder of President John F. Kennedy on November 22, 1963 in Dallas, Texas.

It's not a stretch of the imagination to say that many Americans believe that there was a conspiracy to kill JFK – a conclusion reinforced when a determination was reached by the House Select Committee on Assassinations of the 95th Congress in March 1979. The HSCA's anticlimactic conclusion stated that the President "was probably assassinated as a result of a conspiracy."

The first evidence of a conspiracy, along with a conspiracy theory itself, appeared in Eunice in the form of "Rose Cherami."

Cherami, however, was not a citizen of Eunice.

Rose Cherami was merely the link between Eunice, Louisiana and a possible conspiracy to kill JFK. All JFK "conspiracy theorists" can tie their conspiratorial lineage back to Cherami, as she was the first in line.

She was born Melba Christine Marcades in Texas in 1923.

Ruling out the possibility of clairvoyance and magic bullets, Rose's "prediction" was an indication of foreknowledge. Cherami, as she is known to JFK assassination researchers, stated on Nov. 20, 1963, in Eunice, that the President would be murdered in Dallas on Friday, two days hence. After the assassination, she was also quite possibly the first person to link Lee Harvey Oswald and Jack Ruby.

But few listened to the known prostitute, drug addict and drug trafficker. Those who listen today, and America as a nation, should be haunted by the specter of Rose Cherami.

Who was Rose?

Cherami, according to FBI files and Louisiana State Police records, was known to have over 35 aliases. According to the FBI and various law enforcement reports from dozens of municipalities, these are the various known and recorded aliases of Melba Christine Marcades or Rose Cherami:

Mrs. Albert Rodman
Patsy Sue Allen
Christine Youngblood
Mickey Rodman
Melba Christene
Melba Rodman
Melba Christina Nichols
Rosa Lee Stewart
Zada Marie Johnson
Connie Mackey
Penny Sue Marcades
Zada Lynn Gano
Zada Garacino
Rose Elaine Evans
Marie Stewart
Zada Irene Scars
Zada Marie Green
Rose Elaine Edwards
Roselle Rene Cherami
Rozella Clinkscales
Rose L. Cherami
Rosalie Jeanne Crawford
Connie Mackey
Zada Jano

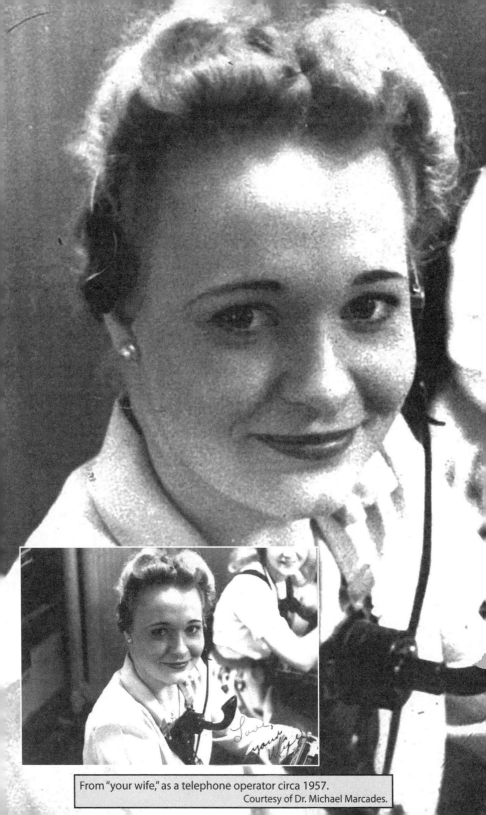

From "your wife," as a telephone operator circa 1957.
Courtesy of Dr. Michael Marcades.

Chapter Two

The Legend Arose

On November 20, 1963, she was Rose Cherami. Rose Cherami found herself in Eunice, more than likely arriving in town from Florida under cover of night, possibly in the late evening of November 19, or in the early morning hours of November 20.

She knew that there was a place called the Silver Slipper, just west of Eunice on Highway 190, on the way to Basile, Louisiana. Rose – who was traveling with two unknown men – made a stop before she planned to leave town, bound for Texas

The Silver Slipper was a bit of a "cathouse" and Rose would find whatever or whomever she might be looking for there. Or indeed, those in need would find her and what she might deliver in the way goods and services.

Rose was not "on the run" so much as she was on *a* run that day of November 20, 1963.

She liked to tell anyone who would listen that she was coming from Florida on this day, and that she was bound for Dallas where she once worked as an exotic dancer at a place called the Carousel Club.

Rose kept company with men that most people spent their lives trying to avoid. By some accounts, she was a "fireball," a woman that no one wanted to handle lest they get burned. Rose found herself on the road, though many times it was a difficult and disparaging road, and it showed in her face.

It's possible that she remembered through her own haze, somewhere from the last half of the 1950s, her own smiling, youthful and cherubic face that adorned a signed photograph to her husband. "Love, your wife" read her own handwriting, when she was a young, wide-eyed telephone operator a lifetime, a son and a husband ago.

Rose knew that she was surviving, as well as she could, as a prostitute and dancer in the grips of a heroin addiction.

After her son was born, she nurtured her own addiction, which drove her away from her husband and family. Her addiction ultimately landed her son, Michael, in the care

Rose and son, Michael, on the day of his christening in 1953.
Courtesy of Dr. Michael Marcades.

of her parents and other family members in another state, another life away from Rose.

When she did visit her son and parents, she tried to be the good housewife, ironing everything in sight during her brief encounters with her family before the highway began to call out her name.

In 1963, however, her face had become less domesticated, swollen and puffy from booze, cigarette-smoky rooms, dope and late night living on the road. The highway, it seemed, was now screaming her name.

On November 20, 1963 Rose found herself on a highway that pulsed like the life blood of this small town of Eunice.

Slicked with autumn rain that day, U.S. Highway 190 wound like an immense king snake through the Louisiana rice fields and over-grown backwoods. Like a magic bullet into the heart of Texas, the "Acadiana Trail" would dart westward, then zigzag across the Lone Star State, from New Orleans and into the realm of history, much like the soon-to-be lore and stories it carried on its asphalt back.

Legend has it that somewhere on this Highway 190 outside of Eunice, a speeding lone vehicle carried two men and, temporarily, one woman named Rose. A man in the backseat physically ejected a flailing, screaming payload from the open door of a moving car.

Perhaps for dramatic effect, Oliver Stone used the depiction of the legend: Rose being thrown from the moving car. Whatever happened may be something else. And whatever happened, Rose hit the ground rolling.

Some locals say that Rose and her road companions were leaving a place called Kilroy's, a "cathouse" just outside of the city limits of Eunice. It was on the east side of U.S. Highway 190, where unsavory characters mingled in the comfort of the secrecy such a place afforded.

Others said that it was the Silver Slipper on the west side of town, along a similar stretch of Highway 190, where the same element gathered just outside the city limits of Eunice.

If the Silver Slipper was "a bit of a cathouse," then Kilroy's was a full-fledged whorehouse.

The right person with the right vice could certainly find whatever they needed readily available at Kilroy's or the Silver Slipper. These were rest stops for weary travelers from New Orleans, bound for Houston or Dallas, who might want to revisit a little of the Big Easy and gamble on some pelvic roulette.

In the haze, something happened at one of the roadside lounges along Highway 190.

According to John H. Davis in *Mafia Kingfish*, a book about New Orleans organized crime figure Carlos Marcello and the JFK assassination: "They had stopped at a roadside bar and restaurant near Eunice. She had gotten a little high, and her companions had abandoned her. The owner of the restaurant then threw her out of his place. While she was trying to hitch a ride, she was grazed by a car and injured slightly. Shortly after that, Lt. Francis Fruge picked her up from the roadside."

While some accounts differ as to whether the incident occurred on the east side or west side of town, the evidence of what Rose said shortly thereafter remained the same.

Did an altercation at the bar resulting in the abandonment of Rose set her in motion to let someone – anyone – know of a devious plot? Was she then, at that point, a woman scorned? Did this motivate her to tell someone about the plot to kill JFK on Friday in Dallas? According to the HSCA report, Rose had been "slapped around" by one of her companions at the Silver Slipper.

Only Rose and the two "Italian looking men" knew what really happened. Perhaps somebody said something they shouldn't have. Perhaps somebody heard something they shouldn't have. Perhaps a phone call Rose made to her family, thus making her companions nervous. Perhaps one of the men made a call and was ordered to ditch Rose, that the mission might not be compromised by her presence or participation in the run.

It is plausible that the assassination run was disguised as a drug run, a prime example of Mafia multi-tasking. There may have been an audible call to shift from the narcotics focus, to have the mechanics, the hired guns, be mindful of only one thing that week: getting the President of the United States.

Rose would have to be left behind for whatever reason.

Perhaps Rose was acting belligerent in public. It would not have been the first time, as her arrest record would reflect. Maybe Rose got high, possibly in the ladies' restroom on some strong heroin, and began nodding off at the bar.

Rose and the two unknown men were certainly not removed from Kilroy's or the Silver Slipper because of her status as a "lady of the night," perhaps betokened by her sobriquet Cherami: "dear friend" in French.

As a prostitute, Rose would have been welcomed at Kilroy's by the owner Hatley Manuel – who was known in town, like a dirty secret in Eunice, as a pimp and a card game "hoss."

In a 2010 interview conducted at his home in Mamou, Louisiana, Hatley (or Hadley depending on who's asking) claimed that he did oversee and manage Kilroy's. After being shown her infamous mugshot picture (see page 72), he also claimed that he did not know Rose, nor had he ever seen her.

Incredibly, he also claimed during the 2010 interview that he had "no idea" who Lee Harvey Oswald was, nor had he ever heard the name of the President's accused assassin.

However, Manuel stated that he did want to get paid for the interview and what he knew. Whatever he knew, Manuel took to the grave with him in 2011.

On November 22, 1963, however, Rose Cherami knew of Eunice's houses of ill-repute, and certainly what had happened to her on November 20.

But that wasn't all she knew. Abandoned by these shady and serious men, Rose might have been the only person ready to tell what she knew to strangers or anyone that might listen. And if she had doubted the truth of her road companions' murderous intentions, the resounding evidence of that truth came like a jolt as she hit the pavement and the side of the highway.

Something must have struck Rose on that afternoon in Eunice, whether it was a moving vehicle, a momentary sense of reason, anger, or the value of life regardless of her own. Perhaps all of these things hit her at once.

In a cloud of opiates, Rose Cherami staggered to her feet from the side of the road. She was possibly bloodied from the scrapes and bruised, and she might have been oblivious to the pick-up truck that struck her.

More than likely, Rose was the source of her own legend, as she later told of how she was "thrown out of a moving vehicle." This way, Rose – who harbored the mind of a junkie and criminal capable of playing the system – would appear as a victim to medical staff and law enforcement. After all, getting hit by a vehicle on the side of the road because she was high on dope was a story that was incriminating and would have garnered less sympathy.

As far as her hell-bent road companions were concerned, Rose Cherami was now someone else's problem on Highway 190. And if Rose was telling the truth, the vehicle that she had been riding in that day reached Dallas later that evening.

Date Admitted	Time	A.M. P.M.	Patient's Name	Address	
11-20-63	11:45	AM	Willard Aguillard	704 N Oak Eunice La
11-20-63	4:00	PM	Rose Cheramie ✓	Thibodaux La
11-20-63	5:30	PM	Linda Lawrence	Eunice La
11-20-63	9:00	PM	Vickie Steven	330 Ida St. Eunice La
11-20-63	9:12	PM	~~Vickie Steven~~	Thibodaux
11-20-63	11:45	PM	Gertrude Young	Eunice La
11-21-63	6:45	AM	Charles Guillory	Rm 147
11-21-63	8:00	AM	Todd Guillory	521 Roosevelt Eunice
11-21-63	10:30	AM	Grace Mills	R. 2B. 28d Eunice
11-21-63	11:00	AM	Edilia Fontenot	R. 2B 761 Eunice
11-21-63	12:40	PM	John Robert Marcantel	Box 72 Basile
11-21-63	4:30	PM	Daryl Drennan	210 So. 8th St Eunice
11-21-63	6:00	PM	Juels Fruelin	R 2 Box 73 Mamou La
11-22-63	1:45	AM	Corine Savoy	141 S St George Eunice
11-22-63	8:00	AM	Corine Savoy	1441 S St. George Eunice
11-22-63	9:00	PM	Stephen Ray Newman	1216 Nixon Eunice
11-22-63	9:30	AM	Mona Johnson	R 2B 175 Basile La
11-22-63	10:30	AM	Elma Manuel	452 N St George Eunice
11-22-63	10:30	AM	Bridget Francois	R 2B 274 Church Point
11-22-63	11:00	PM	Alica Mitchell	1150 N Junction Eunice
11-22-63	9:00	PM	Ernie Buckhorn	492 ... Church Point
11-23-63	10:30	PM	Margaret Whittington	612 East 5th St Eunice
11-23-63	1:50	AM	mrs Mike Shehotole	1104 8th St manor
11-23-63	8:30	PM	William Savage	Room 131 Eunice

Photocopy of Moosa Hospital ER register, the only proof of Rose in Eunice, with Rose's signature by her own hand. Note the spelling of the last name ending with an "i" and not "ie," as recorded in the HSCA findings.

Courtesy of Louis Pavur

Chapter Three

The Register

It was a Wednesday in Eunice at the local hospital, but it would not be a typical Wednesday. Unbeknown to the staff at the Moosa Hospital, the week was shaping up to be one of the worst in American history.

Louis Pavur, a now retired radiologic technologist, recalled in a 2012 interview with the *Eunice News* that he was working at the now-defunct Moosa Hospital on November 20, 1963, offering his assistance to the late Dr. J.T. Thompson and a nurse Broussard.

"It wasn't often that we got someone thrown out of a car brought into the hospital. I worked near the emergency room and thought the doctor might need some X-rays taken," Pavur recalled. "I was present in the Emergency Room when they brought Rose Cherami in. I saw a woman with dark hair who was wearing blue jeans and a white T-shirt, who was not bruised up and did not meet the description of someone who needed x-rays."

Pavur said that he remembers Cherami and that day well.

"I remember that she said that she was thrown out of an automobile and they called Dr. J.T. Thompson, and I was in the emergency room," Pavur said. "She was a short woman with an average build. This woman claimed she was thrown out of a car, but I didn't really see any severe evidence of that. I did not hear her say, specifically, that Kennedy would be assassinated. The police took her off to the Eunice City Jail, and it wasn't un-

The old Moosa Hospital in Eunice, Louisiana as it looked in 1963.
Photo courtesy of J. Richard DesHotels.

til a couple of days later, the day of the assassination, that it had come out that she had predicted it."

In other words, Pavur said, when the President was killed, many in the hospital remembered "that woman" who said something about the murder of JFK – which she said was going to happen on that Friday. Pavur said that the staff at Moosa Hospital in Eunice treated her for her bruises and scrapes and determined she had suffered no real trauma from her ordeal.

One of Pavur's prized belongings is a photocopy of the original emergency room register with Cherami's signature, in which she listed Thibodaux, LA as her address. Cherami signed herself in at 4:00 P.M. according to Pavur's copied document.

"I thought it was a significant part of history, it's a piece of history," Pavur said. "I thought it would be an interesting something to look at one day. I didn't how deep it was going to go, or the extent of the investigation."

Pavur said that he knew the time was right to make a copy of the emergency room register when FBI, government officials, or men flashing such credentials, came to Eunice and took medical records from Moosa and an arrest record on Rose from the Eunice Police Department.

"That's when I found out that she had predicted that Kennedy would be assassinated, when they came to the hospital and did all of this stuff," Pavur said. "After that, I said 'Jesus! I'm going to get a copy of that.' That happened so many years ago, I can't remember what happened to the original emergency room register."

Pavur said that also present at the Moosa hospital that afternoon of November 20, 1963 was the late L.G. Carrier, at the time with the Eunice Police Department. Pavur said he remembered Carrier arriving shortly after Cherami was brought in. Jane Carrier, widow of L.G. Carrier, said that her husband related to her that he overheard the radio report about Cherami and then went to the hospital.

Mrs. Carrier said that he also told her about FBI agents visiting Eunice "within days" after the Kennedy assassination. "They came a very short time later and picked up all the records. L.G. told me that they came and took her records from Moosa and from the jail." Mrs. Carrier said that her late husband was one of the few locals who actually heard Cherami speak of a plot to kill Kennedy.

"Nobody bothered investigating, they all thought she was a nut case," Mrs. Carrier said. "At the time they probably didn't know that she worked with Jack Ruby. And that's probably where she overheard something about the plot to kill Kennedy."

Ruby, a Dallas night club owner and a man who was affiliated with Chicago and New Orleans organized crime lords, killed Oswald on live television, as the suspected assassin was being led from Dallas city jail to the county jail two days after Kennedy was assassinated on Friday.

Louis Pavur believes that JFK was assassinated as the result of a conspiracy. Pavur said that he did not believe that Lee Harvey Oswald, a New Orleans native, had shot Kennedy, mainly because Pavur's sister worked in a New Orleans department store with Oswald's mother, and Oswald was often around the store. "She said that Oswald was 'too stupid to get out of the rain,'" Pavur said. "She said he would just get lost in the department store. That he just wasn't smart."

As for this strange patient named Rose Cherami, apparent "narcotics withdrawals" or some strange symptoms associated with drugs made this woman a candidate for the drunk tank at the Eunice jail.

"We didn't know if she was drunk or hopped up when she was talking to us in the Emergency Room. She was talking kind of out of her head when she was talking to us," Pavur said. "I assume that it was why she was released to the Eunice Police Department."

The emergency room entrance in 2013. It was on November 20, 1963 at 4 p.m. that Rose signed the emergency room register. This is possibly the first place that she mentioned the foreknowledge of an assassination attempt on JFK.
Photo by Todd C. Elliott.

Such strange, drug-fiend behavior triggered a hospital staffer to contact Lt. Francis Fruge of the Louisiana State Police. According to both research, and his own sworn testimony, a hospital worker from Moosa phoned Fruge in regards to Rose.

Whether he picked her up on the side of the highway or at the hospital, Rose was in his custody now. It would be his responsibility to move Rose Cherami from the hospital to the Eunice jail.

A budding Rose in the 1940s.
Photo courtesy of Dr. Michael Marcades.

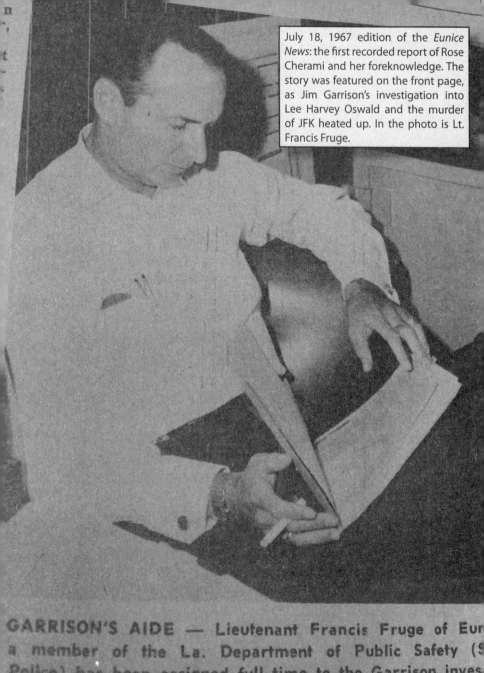

July 18, 1967 edition of the *Eunice News*: the first recorded report of Rose Cherami and her foreknowledge. The story was featured on the front page, as Jim Garrison's investigation into Lee Harvey Oswald and the murder of JFK heated up. In the photo is Lt. Francis Fruge.

GARRISON'S AIDE — Lieutenant Francis Fruge of Eur a member of the La. Department of Public Safety (S Police) has been assigned full time to the Garrison inves tion by Col. Thomas Burbank, director. Lt. Fruge has on narcotic investigation work, which led directly into Kennedy assassination study when a woman picked up in nice turned out to be a former employe of Jack Ruby. ever, who is another dead witness. Lt. Fruge is checkin other leads and reports to Garrison each week.

Chapter Four

Meanwhile Back at the Eunice Jail

L
t. Francis Fruge of the Louisiana State Police was from a
smaller town west of Eunice called Basile.
During his routine highway patrol up and down U.S.
Highway 190, he probably remembered the policeman's ball,
scheduled for that evening of November 20, 1963.

Fruge was invited to attend. However, his festivities would
be cut short by Rose.

When Fruge first met Rose Cherami is unknown. Fruge had
probably encountered Rose at one point or another along U.S.
Highway 190, as it was his routine to patrol the highway, investigating various prostitutes and drug-runners. That day, anyone who
saw a distraught Rose on the side of the highway probably cringed
and knew something was highly unusual about the situation.

Chris Mills, a British writer, detailed a Fruge-Cherami encounter in his essay entitled "Rambling Rose." Mills wrote that
Fruge happened upon "a woman who seemed to be the victim
of a road traffic accident. Although she did not seem badly injured Fruge thought it prudent to take her to the Moosa Hospital in Eunice to be examined. During the journey the woman
told Fruge that her name was Rose Cheramie [sic], explaining
that she was en-route from Miami to Houston via Dallas."

According to Mills, Fruge brought Cherami to the Moosa
Hospital. Fruge's testimony before the HSCA hearings in 1978
stated that someone from the Moosa Hospital called him in to
take responsibility for Rose – who was already in their care and
showed signs of being a raving drug addict under the influence.

Though nothing can be confirmed, allegedly a man by the
name of Frank Odom picked Rose up on the side of Highway

190 in his truck after nearly grazing her with his vehicle. Allegedly, Odom drove her to Moosa Hospital and left her there. Perhaps Odom was even the first to hear Rose and her rambling about an assassination. I was unable to interview Odom. Eunice residents, along with Odom family members, confirmed in 2010 that Mr. Frank Odom had been long dead. According to H.P. Albarelli's book, *A Secret Order: Investigating the High Strangeness and Synchronicity in the JFK Assassination,* Odom alleged that Cherami cursed him out "something fierce" for the duration of the ride to the hospital.

Regardless of who took her to Moosa Hospital, Cherami was transported to Moosa after being found on the side of the road.

There is merely circumstantial evidence as to who took her to the hospital, or which side of the highway she was on. The fact is that at 4 P.M. she had signed the emergency room register at the Moosa Hospital as "Rose Cherami" on November 20, 1963. On the register, Rose listed her address: "Thibodaux, Louisiana."

From Moosa, Fruge was the one who was tasked with escorting Rose to the Eunice city jail. After a brief stay she was committed to the East Louisiana State Hospital in Jackson upon the recommendation of Dr. F.J. DeRouen – who was assistant coroner of St. Landry Parish.

Before committing Rose to a state hospital, Dr. DeRouen allegedly first met her that day in the Eunice city jail. He was called to the jail because the police reported to him that they had a woman in the jail who had begun to act irrationally and violently.

According to documentation found within Jim Garrison's National Archives on Rose, "she appeared to suffer severe narcotic withdrawals" while at the hospital. Rose was "taken to jail and given a sedative but she soon became agitated, stripped off her clothing and slashed her ankles."

Rose purportedly cut her ankles with her fingernails and then proceeded to scratch the walls of the jail cell, bloodying her fingertips and nails.

Is it possible that Rose was faking her symptoms to get a transfer to the state mental institution? Was this just another example of her criminal mind working, playing the system?

In a 2012 interview with the *Eunice News*, Dr. DeRouen said that he did not remember much: not seeing Rose Cherami at all, seeing any female patient acting irrationally or violent, giving a sedative that caused an adverse reaction, hearing a patient mention a plot to murder JFK, nor transferring any woman to the East Louisiana State Hospital.

Dr. DeRouen also could not remember that he had determined that Cherami was a heroin addict of about nine years, who had shot her last intravenous cocktail at about 2 P.M. that day.

Although DeRouen did not remember Rose Cherami, he did not deny treating her. He said that due to a recent stroke, his memory was not what it used to be. "If you say that I did those things, then I must have done them," Dr. DeRouen said at his Eunice home in that interview with the *Eunice News*. "I just have a hard time remembering that time in my life."

However, Dr. DeRouen said (like most Americans in regards to the watershed moment) that he remembered the Friday that Kennedy was assassinated, and that he had been in his office on 2nd Street in downtown Eunice. He also remembered that he was not a fan of President Kennedy.

When asked about Rose babbling some plot to kill Kennedy in Dallas, DeRouen denounced it as the symptoms of narcotic withdrawal and blamed the drugs that she was on at the time.

But no drug has a documented side-effect of making a user able to point to a time and place where a person, in this case the leader of the free world, would be murdered.

As Dr. DeRouen struggled with his memory in 2012, an anonymous Eunice resident disclosed that the doctor's memory trouble following his stroke may have been a ruse. The reliable source, well versed in the Eunice connection with the Rose Cherami incident, said that he had questioned Dr. DeRouen in the late 1990s prior to his stroke. The source said that Dr. De-Rouen volunteered no information back then either.

If there was no raving, drug addled, female inmate at the Eunice city Jail, then how did Rose end up in one of the biggest state mental facilities in the area, hours before JFK would be cut down?

Better question: why?

Was it something she said?

Chapter Five

Going to Jackson

The late Lt. Francis Fruge was, without a doubt, the man who was tasked with driving Rose to the East Louisiana State Hospital – which was a state mental facility in Jackson, Louisiana.

Fruge found himself summoned back to the Eunice jail from his festive evening at the policeman's ball. And he was, perhaps, the first to hear Cherami's strange tale in detail, about how President Kennedy would be killed in two days in Dallas by the men with whom she traveled.

So that evening of November 20, 1963, Lt. Francis Fruge was called back in to the Eunice jail, allegedly some time after 10:30 P.M. He was to accompany the mess that was Rose Cherami to the Jackson hospital. Indeed, he would drive her all the way there. And by the time they would get her admitted the hospital, it would be November 21, 1963.

Fruge drove her to the state hospital, nearly a two-hour drive to the east. Fruge would testify before the House Select Committee on Assassinations on April 18, 1978, that during this pivotal time frame, "She related to me that she was coming from Florida to Dallas with two men who were Italians or resembled Italians. They had stopped at this lounge and they'd had a few drinks ... and had gotten into an argument or something. The manager of the lounge threw her out and she got on the road and hitchhiked to catch a ride, and this is when she got hit by a vehicle." The lounge Rose Cherami spoke of, Fruge stated, was indeed the Silver Slipper, a house of prostitution.

Fruge further testified that upon questioning her of her business in Dallas: "She said she was going to, number one, pick up some money, pick up her baby, and to kill Kennedy."

And perhaps after hearing such an astounding statement coming from the back seat on a nearly two-hour drive that night, the only sound would be the hum of the engine on the highway, as eyeballs shifted to the rear-view mirror after Rose gave her "word from the underground" to Fruge.

Perhaps Lt. Francis Fruge and Rose Cherami locked eyes for a second or two in that rear-view mirror. Maybe it was the thunderous silence of disbelief that permeated the night air on a lonely highway in Louisiana.

It's not impossible that, at that moment, lightning flashed in the distance, sealing their destiny.

Flashing forward to 1978 before the HSCA, Lt. Francis Fruge would recall that Rose Cherami, when relating these stories to him, seemed quite lucid.

Records indicate that Cherami would be in for her second visit to this state hospital in Jackson. Previously, she was institutionalized for being "criminally insane" on July 13, 1961, according to Louisiana State Police and FBI records.

This time Cherami was taken to the same hospital – which Lee Harvey Oswald had applied for employment just months prior in Summer of 1963. The day after she was admitted, Kennedy was murdered in Dealey Plaza in Dallas.

In her book *A Farewell to Justice*, Joan Mellen described Cherami's stay in the state mental hospital (p. 206):

"On Friday, November 22nd, at twenty minutes before noon, Rose was watching television in the hospital recreation area. Scenes in Dallas flashed on the screen. President Kennedy was on his way.

"'Somebody's got to do something!' Cherami shouted. 'They're going to kill the president!' No one paid any attention. The motorcade pulled into view. 'Watch!' Rose cried out. 'This is when it's going to happen! They're going to get him! They're going to get him at the underpass!'"

Shots rang out in Dallas.

A phone rang in the Jackson state hospital. Rattled by the shooting of JFK in Dallas, Fruge frantically called the hospital to get Cherami back in State Police custody. He allegedly told the staff not to release her until he arrived. However, he was told by hospital staff that he could not collect or question Cherami until Monday.

As he waited, Fruge allegedly called the FBI in Lafayette, Louisiana, who told him the case was closed and that they already had their man. By Monday, the world would know the names of Lee Harvey Oswald and Jack Ruby.

On Monday, according to his HSCA deposition, Fruge was finally able to question Cherami, who spoke of how "two men traveling with her from Miami were going to Dallas to kill the President. For her part, Cherami was to obtain $8,000 from an unidentified source in Dallas and proceed to Houston with the two men to complete a drug deal."

Cherami was also supposed to pick up her little boy, her son Michael, from her parents, who had been looking after him.

Cherami told Fruge details of the pending drug transaction in Houston. She said reservations had been made at the Rice Hotel in Houston, but she didn't say who made them. The trio – which consisted of Rose and the two Italian-looking men – was to meet a seaman who was bringing eight kilos of heroin to Galveston by boat. Cherami had the name of the seaman and the boat he was arriving on. Once the drug deal was complete, the trio would travel to Mexico.

Fruge was encouraged by his supervisors to follow up on the leads. Cherami was taken into the custody of Lt. Fruge one last time. Along with Louisiana State Trooper Wayne Morein (who would later become the Sheriff of Evangeline Parish in Louisiana), the two became part of the first non-publicized investigation into the murder of President Kennedy.

On Nov. 28, 1963, Fruge, Morein and Cherami took a plane to Texas, after contacting the chief customs agent in Galveston regarding the boat and the seaman with purported heroin. The chief customs agent in Galveston reportedly verified the docking schedule of the boat and the name of the seaman. The seaman was never captured or detained, as customs allegedly botched the tailing of the seaman, who escaped. Soon after, U.S. Customs closed the case, according to Fruge's deposition.

Fruge also stated that during the flight to Houston, Cherami laughed out loud at one of the headlines she read in the daily paper. The headlines indicated that Ruby and Oswald had never known one another and had never seen each other before the shooting of Oswald.

According to Cherami, she had worked for Jack Ruby, or "Pinky," as she knew him, at his nightclub in Dallas, and Ruby and Oswald "had been shacking up for years"; they were "bedmates."

Whether Rose alluded to Ruby and Oswald being homosexual lovers is unknown. It's possible that Rose meant that they were "in the same bed" as far as plotters might be, in a manner of speaking.

She mentioned that she once worked as a stripper at a club Ruby owned known as the Pink Door.

Years later, according to an anonymous Eunice source, this would become well known to certain members of Jim Garrison's investigative team, who purported that the Silver Slipper in Eunice was owned by none other than Jack Ruby. It was further alleged by Cherami that Carlos Marcello, organized crime boss of New Orleans, fronted Ruby the money to open the Silver Slipper.

There are no records found, however, to prove any of these allegations.

But when the plane carrying Rose Cherami touched down in Houston on Monday after the assassination, Fruge contacted the Dallas Police Department. He told Capt. Will Fritz that he had a suspect in custody who was in Houston and could testify as a witness that Ruby and Oswald had known each other. Fruge seemed eager to help in the investigation: to deliver this important Rose Cherami to the Dallas Police's doorstep.

According to Fruge's testimony, Capt. Fritz said he wasn't interested in Rose. Captain Fritz said that he had dropped his investigation.

Now, it seemed, so did the Louisiana State Police. Fruge suggested that Cherami speak to federal authorities.

But after she was denied by the Dallas Police Department, Cherami refused to talk to the FBI and claimed to "not want to get involved in this mess." Perhaps she was motivated by fear not to speak with the FBI. As the strange events of the assassination unfolded, who wouldn't be afraid?

As America and the world struggled to make sense of the shifting events in Dallas, maybe it had just dawned on Rose what the magnitude of the ordeal was and how big it could get. Maybe she realized her life might already be in danger, and she knew better than to tell anyone at the FBI.

According to Fruge, all of the information on the narcotics ring operating in and out of Louisiana that was given to him by Cherami was verified as true and good information. Even the Rice Hotel reservation made for her under a fake name checked out. Perhaps Ruby had made the reservations at the Rice Hotel in Houston.

No matter, for it was in Houston that trooper Morein and Lt. Fruge said their good-byes to Rose Cherami. She was left in Houston, unofficially extradited back to Texas, it seemed, without a paper trail. Rather than being a headache for the Louisiana State Police, Rose would become someone else's problem in Houston.

It was the last time Fruge would see her alive.

As elements of a plot that seemed to originate from New Orleans began to come to light years later, Fruge was part of a team of investigators probing the JFK assassination with Jim Garrison, the New Orleans District Attorney and the only person to ever bring a trial in the murder of President Kennedy.

In 1967 Fruge – who was working as a Garrison aide investigating the Rose Cherami lead – visited the Silver Slipper in Eunice. He allegedly showed the owner, Mac Manual, some photographs of men suspected to be traveling with Rose on that fateful day in 1963.

Fruge testified to having shown Manual two mug shots of men that he identified as the two mystery men who traveled with Rose. The owner claimed that the two men had been to the Silver Slipper before, allegedly transporting prostitutes from Florida to Eunice, but he did not know them by name. Fruge claimed that the man had identified Sergio Arcacha-Smith, an anti-Castro Cuban expatriate with ties to the CIA, and another Cuban man known only to Fruge as "Osanto."

A conversation about Rose was documented on July 18, 1967, when the *Eunice News'* Matt Vernon (writer of the Comment Cava column) reported perhaps the first news of "Melba Christine Marcades" (aka Rose Cherami) who was "a one-time performer in Jack Ruby's nightclub" in a brief interview of Lt. Francis Fruge.

According to the article, Cherami "told Francis that Oswald and Ruby were close friends for years. She was found dead on the side of a Texas highway September 4, 1965 … she would have been an important witness except that she was, like 23 or more other potential witnesses, dead. Despite her unsavory reputation and record, everything she told Francis … checked out." Francis Fruge said he thought Cherami could have had direct knowledge of the assassination plot.

While other research and writings asserted that Fruge and Morein embarked upon the first, non-publicized murder investigation in the assassination of JFK, Morein would not confirm this. In both 2010 and 2012, Morein declined to comment on the matter. Morein only confirmed that he did once work with Fruge.

Francis Fruge

Chapter Six

GOOD DOCTOR, BAD DOCTOR

One doctor – whose name continues to circulate within the saga of Rose Cherami – was mentioned in the HSCA report as the source of the report of Rose's foreknowledge, as it was allegedly told to staff members of the East Louisiana State Hospital.

His statements shoot holes in the validity of the published HSCA findings. Dr. Donn E. Bowers, now of Mississippi, said that the sworn testimony of Dr. Victor Weiss is inaccurate.

Bowers said that he took issue with page 200 and 201 of Appendix 10 to the House Select Committee on Assassinations, which stated:

"The commission [sic] interviewed one of the doctors on staff at the East Louisiana State Hospital who had seen Cheramie(sic) during her stay there at the time of the Kennedy assassination. The doctor corroborated aspects of [the Cherami allegations]. Dr. Victor Weiss verified that he was employed as a resident physician at the hospital in 1963. He recalled that on Monday, November 25, 1963, he was asked by another physician, Dr. Bowers, to see a patient who had been committed November 20 or 21. Dr. Bowers allegedly told Weiss that the patient, Rose Cheramie, [sic] had stated before the assassination that President Kennedy was going to be killed."

Bowers said that he was not even at the Jackson Hospital when Rose was committed. While he did work at the Jackson hospital on weekends to earn extra money, Bowers said that at the time when Rose was admitted, he was in New Orleans working at the Southern Baptist Hospital.

Bowers also said that he was never called to testify in the 1970s during the HSCA investigations as a possible key witness, and a source of the story of Rose Cherami and her foreknowledge among the staff at the East Louisiana State Hospital in Jackson.

While he asserts that he never saw Rose Cherami in the East Louisiana State Hospital, he is one of the only people to review and look at the medical files from her second stint at Jackson, a luxury afforded to him being a physician that had worked at the hospital.

Nothing about any foreknowledge of JFK's impending murder was in the file, according to a 2013 interview.

Bowers contends that Dr. Weiss was the one who told him the strange tale of Rose Cherami during a dove-hunting excursion on the Sunday following the President's murder on Friday. When he read the published report of the HSCA in 1979, Bowers was prompted to make a phone call.

"When all of this started coming out, I finally called (Dr. Weiss)," Bowers said. "He was in practice in San Antonio then, in the practice of psychiatry. Once he finished at East Louisiana State Hospital, he took up his practice in San Antonio. And I called him and said, 'Vic, you told me that story about Rose, but I was not there on the admission. And I never was.'"

Bowers said that Weiss "seemed like he was embarrassed" and said, "Well, I was confused, I guess. I didn't really remember the facts right."

Bowers said that Weiss "mumbled a lot" into the phone. "And that was the end of the conversation," Bowers said. "He was embarrassed that he had said that. You know, psychiatrists don't like to be wrong in their thoughts."

Bowers said that he had no idea if Weiss was lying about not remembering the facts correctly.

"I never understood why he thought that," Bowers said. "In fact, when I challenged him. I could only take it to mean that he was embarrassed that he had made an incorrect assumption that I was present at the admission of Rose Cherami. So, I didn't follow up anymore. And he died not too long after that. I think he had prostate cancer and died of that. I never did talk to him again because he didn't seem to want to talk about it."

Judyth Vary Baker, author of *Me & Lee* – an account of her relationship with Lee Harvey Oswald during the spring and summer of 1963 – said that the Jackson hospital was the site of a "cancer soup" weapon test on live human subjects, prisoners of Louisiana State Penitentiary, a prison farm in Angola, Louisiana.

Baker contended that Oswald (in concert with David Ferrie) was part of a project at Jackson and covered his plausible appearance at the hospital by requesting, or filling out, an application for employment at the Hospital on the day he observed a subject's exposure to the cancer weapon, which was being tested for a future assassination attempt on Fidel Castro in Cuba.

Baker also said that Oswald was affiliated with Carlos Marcello through Oswald's uncle, Dutz Murret, who allegedly worked for Marcello in a bookkeeper role.

In regards to Rose's files at East Louisiana State Hospital, Dr. Bowers stated that he looked over at least one of Rose's files at the hospital and found nothing unusual about it except for the fact that Rose was admitted into the hospital, then released back into the custody of Lt. Frances Fruge and the Louisiana State Police.

"You'd think that that was not the right place for her to, for them to take her back," Bowers said. "Because I don't know what they did with her."

When told that Rose – who was an admitted hospital patient in a state mental facility – was seemingly "extradited" back to Texas, as she was left in Houston never to return to a doctor's care, Bowers said that "struck him as odd."

Bowers said that he recalled where he was the day and the moment JFK was shot in Dealey Plaza. He was in the cafeteria at Southern Baptist Hospital in New Orleans having a lunch of red beans and rice.

When asked if he thought that Carlos Marcello had something to do with JFK's assassination, Bowers answered, "Well, I'll tell you this, Carlos Marcello was a very, very powerful Mafioso, there's no question about that," he said. "And the way they ran things [in New Orleans], he could have and would have done anything."

Chapter Seven

Little Big Mamou

Rose was considered a low-ranking member of the Carlos Marcello heroin network – which worked in unison with another crime boss, Santos "Sam" Trafficante, who controlled the Florida market, according to Lamar Waldron, author of *Legacy of Secrecy*: "It's ironic that a woman who was one of the lowest members of Marcello's crime empire came close to saving JFK's life, and on at least three occasions would risk her own life to help law enforcement."

Alluding to organized crime figures in the Eunice area in 1963 is one thing. Proof to place them in the area is another thing entirely.

When theories and hypotheses won't do, a visit must be paid to the Holiday Lounge in Mamou, Louisiana.

There's a shot of proof in that 55-year-old lounge that looked as if it had remained intact, unhindered by time, since 1963, with the evident decor and vintage, worn furniture. At one time, it was the happening spot, with half of the building serving as a restaurant.

The place in 2013 belonged to Eugene Manuel and his mother, Linda – who, like Rose, was born in Houston and lived in Cocoa Beach, Florida at one time. However, Linda would have been younger than Rose, and she claimed that she did not know her or recognize her photographs.

Growing up in the bar, or being involved in his family's business from an early age, Eugene said that in the late 1970s or early 1980s, he took a phone call one day at the Holiday Lounge. It was for his father, Edison Manuel, or "Tee-Ed" as he was known, and still is today in Mamou. The man on the phone stated that he was Carlos Marcello.

A disbelieving teenager, Eugene laughed it off as a prank call and went to get his father to tell him that there was a man on the phone who said that he was Carlos Marcello. Eugene recalled that his father gave him a serious, stern look.

"He looked mad," Eugene said. "By his face, I knew something was wrong. He said, 'What are you doing? Don't talk to him like that. Give me the phone.'"

"Well, daddy ... you think ... " Eugene said, still not believing that he had just been on the phone with Marcello.

"Yeah, that's him," his father said.

Eugene said that his father explained to him after he got off the telephone. "He said to me, 'the next time that man calls, you don't ask questions, you don't pick at him. He's not an ugly man, he's a nice man," Eugene said.

Then Eugene said that his father asked him, "What if he got mad at you?"

It was at that moment that Eugene said that he became enlightened about the closeness of the shadowy underworld in his small town of Mamou.

A worried look ran across his father's face that seemed to say, "What the hell did you say to him?" In a 2013 interview,

HOLIDAY LOUNGE-MAMOU, LA.
since 1958

Edison "Tee Ed" Manuel

1962

Photos courtesy of J. Richard DesHotels.

Eugene said that his father "had a friendship" with Marcello, but that his old man never had any business dealings with Carlos.

However, back in 1963, he said, the Holiday Lounge was filled with slot machines and a jukebox purchased from "a middle man" that Eugene believed had some affiliation with the Pelican Novelty Company, out of New Orleans, owned by Marcello.

However, the Pelican Novelty Company was one of three companies started by the big daddy of the underworld, the "Prime Minister," Frank Costello. Costello was of the infamous "five families" of Italian organized crime which originated in New York.

Research has shown that shortly after meeting with Governor Huey P. Long in the early 1930s, Costello began shipping slot machines to Louisiana in droves. Legend has it that, as per Long's deal with Costello, Louisiana would get a 10-percent cut of "the take." Long would ironically meet with a public assassination, much like JFK, in which the alleged assassin was also silenced shortly after, again as in JFK's murder. Dr Seymour Weiss was Huey P. Long's accused assassin.

There were so many slot machines in Louisiana at the time, Eugene said, that behind the Holiday Lounge and Restaurant, his father built some single-rooms for some of the traveling slot machine and jukebox technicians, possibly affiliated with Marcello. Everyone in Eunice and Mamou seem to have common knowledge that these motel rooms were considered "cathouses."

Eugene denied this as gossip and rumor.

"I'm not saying that nobody never got a piece of ass in those rooms," he said. "I just use it as storage today." The rooms still stand, overgrown with weeds, vines and spider webs.

His mother, Linda, said that she had met with Carlos Marcello, even having dinner with him in New Orleans. She described him as a "nice, regular guy." The men in Marcello's circle of friends talked amongst themselves, she said, the wives knew very little as to what was discussed or where and how money might flow.

Eugene offered more about the town often dubbed "Big Mamou."

Mamou is a sleepy, prairie Cajun village within Evangeline Parish, just about 9 miles north of Eunice up La. Hwy 13. Mamou is known for its traditional rooster- or chicken-chasing Mardi Gras, and boasts a population of about 3,500 people.

The four cotton gins that were once the life blood of Mamou are long gone. It seems an unlikely place for a major, organized crime boss to go to a hospital. However, Eugene said that Marcello would regularly drive to the Mamou Hospital for treatment by a world-class surgeon, Dr. Frank Savoy, Jr.

Savoy and his father built the hospital in the country, after graduating from LSU Health Medical School in New Orleans. In 1950 they opened Savoy Hospital with eight beds and later expanded to 185 beds, becoming the Savoy Medical Center.

New Orleans is where Dr. Savoy first met Marcello as a patient, according to Eugene Manuel. The doctor apparently had a reputation for being one of the best. Marcello, like any crime boss, would want nothing but the best.

Eugene said that he remembers seeing a long, black limousine at the hospital one day, complete with a Negro chauffeur waiting in the car. Eugene said that he was told by one of Dr. Savoy's sons that the limo belonged to Carlos Marcello.

Dr. Savoy passed away in 2010. Bobby Savoy, the 89-year old widow of Dr. Savoy, lives in Eunice. She passed away in January 2014, after the original publication of this book.

During a 2013 interview, when asked if her husband treated Carlos Marcello of New Orleans, without hesitation she confirmed

Savoy Hospital in Mamou, Louisiana.
Courtesy of J. Richard DesHotels.

Eugene's story. However, within the same breath, she winced and said, "Oh wait, Carlos? Was it Carlos? No, I'm not sure."

After asking her daughter, who was present in an adjoining room in her Eunice home, about Carlos Marcello, the daughter sprang into action and reminded her about Carlos Marcello being a dangerous man.

Her daughter claimed that Marcello is a dangerous man, as opposed to using the past tense. She must have meant Marcello "was a dangerous man," as he died in March of 1993 in his Metairie, Louisiana home.

Even in death, the Marcello name retains an edge of fear.

Finally, the widow Savoy arrived at the name "Sam Roselli." She was sure of it; this "Sam Roselli" of New Orleans was a patient of her late husband.

She stated that her husband was never friends with Marcello. However, she did say that she met a really nice man who showed up one day at the hospital in Mamou in a limo, but she just couldn't recall the name. "In fact, there so many limos in and out of the hospital back then," said the widow Savoy.

She said that she thought that she should have a limo as well, just to keep up with the latest automobile standards in Mamou.

Was it possible that Carlos Marcello visited a country hospital in the middle of Mamou? And was it a likely place for a "made man" to go to the hospital?

Perhaps the country hospital afforded a boss like Marcello some privacy. Perhaps if he went into a hospital in New Orleans, the press and enemies might find out and sense a weakness in the Godfather of Louisiana. It's possible that the hospital, with the central location of Mamou in the state, provided a meeting ground for Mafia figures from Texas. For Marcello, having the best surgeon in the state would have been an added bonus.

Mrs. Savoy said that her husband had patients who would travel from all over the state. She added that he even had patients who would come from Washington, D.C. and Florida.

Eugene said that Dr. Savoy was a friend of Marcello, like his own father. He further stated that with whores and prostitutes in the area, regular health screenings and treatments were administered to "the girls" by Dr. Savoy.

The "shaky" verification of Bobby Savoy would prompt an interview with a Mrs. Carina "Sue" Vasser of Mamou.

"T'aunt Sue" (which means "Aunt Sue" in French) was the name that everyone in Mamou and Eunice knew her by. And her reputation for being an ambassador of sorts for the town of Mamou was known all over the world, it would seem.

Vasser is the owner and operator of a small, yet world-renowned, bar called Fred's, which had been around since 1963. In a 2013 interview, Vasser said that Marcello was definitely in and out of Mamou. Marcello even went to her bar one time.

After all, she said, her son Jimmy married the daughter of Carlos Marcello.

Vasser jokingly referred to herself as having "Mafia grandchildren." She said that her grandchildren – who were now successful in life, with one being a lawyer and the other a doctor – just happen to live in or work in the Dallas, Texas area today. She said that her son and Carlos Marcello's daughter moved to Dallas years ago. According to Vasser, they were still married.

The importance of these accounts is that they are proof of a mob presence in the Eunice and Mamou area. The organized crime figures would then have taken U.S. Highway 190 to Eunice from New Orleans before turning north on Louisiana State Highway 13 to Mamou. This could place Marcello associates in Eunice and perhaps even present an opportunity for real estate investments, slot machine sales and jukebox distribution.

The underworld presence is thus proven in Eunice in 1963.

And Rose Cherami, as described in *Mafia Kingfish* by John H. Davis, was "an underworld hanger-on" (p. 607). By this description, if Rose had any business with any organized crime in Louisiana, as she did, then it would have been Marcello's. If she were "hanging on" to any part of the underworld, it was Marcello's.

Marcello has figured in the JFK assassination conspiracy as a key component because of the fact that Marcello did not lack a motive to gladly assist in the killing of JFK. After being deported by Robert Kennedy and the U.S. Justice Department to Guatemala in 1961, Marcello had his motive. While in prison, Marcello himself allegedly admitted to being a participant in the assassination of JFK.

Edward T. Haslam describes the scenario in *Dr. Mary's Monkey* (p. 342):

"Bobby Kennedy was at war with the Mafia and was prosecuting organized crime figures in record numbers. His primary target was Carlos Marcello. Kennedy openly said that he would use underworld tactics to fight the underworld. He had Marcello kidnapped and dropped him in Guatemala without a U.S. passport. Marcello was so powerful that he was able to get back into the United States without a passport, and despite pressure against him by the U.S. Attorney General."

The "underworld tactics" that Bobby Kennedy spoke of might possibly include placing "moles," or informants, in the circles of Marcello's power.

Haslam suggests in his book that RFK may have been taking note of known Marcello-connected politicians who began to show interest in a New Orleans native who was believed to be

FROM LEFT TO RIGHT: Mr. and Mrs. Carlos Marcello, Jackie Marcello (bride), Preston "Jimmy" Dugas (groom), Sue and Earl Vasser.

Picture courtesy of "Tante" Sue Carina Vasser

a defector to Russia. There was a man who needed to get back from the U.S.S.R. with his family. The man who might possibly be RFK's mole, Haslam theorized in *Dr. Mary's Monkey*, was Lee Harvey Oswald.

It should be noted that after his brother was killed, Bobby Kennedy remained the Attorney General for a brief time. However, the "top cop" in the land was suddenly quiet. Bobby Kennedy said nothing publicly about investigating his own brother's murder, nor seemed to pursue an investigation. Even though he could have afforded to fund his own private crusade to seek out his brother's killers, with access to information in the halls of power, he did nothing.

RFK even seemed to cease his war on organized crime overnight.

Why?

Haslam asks the question: "Was Lee Harvey Oswald chosen because accusing him would neutralize Bobby?"

Rose could have been, on some lower level, much like the pawn Oswald.

During her flight to Houston with Fruge and Morein that Monday after the assassination, perhaps it was not that Rose refused out of fear to tell the FBI of what she knew about the plan to kill JFK. Perhaps Rose had already told the FBI of what she knew.

If so, Rose might have clearly seen the bigger picture of things that were unfolding during the time following the assassination, while most Americans were still trying to figure it out.

Chapter Eight

HER LIFE AND HER LIFE OF CRIME

There can be no real biography of Rose Cherami, it seems. Or perhaps there are two biographies of Cherami: one of her life and one of her life of crime.

Her story exists in her criminal record with a "rap sheet" spanning FBI files, Louisiana State Police records, other various municipal arrest records, her death certificate, medical records and the yet-to-be-written stories of those who are still alive to remember her or those who chose to forget during the time of this writing.

She exists today as an enigma, riddled in mystery.

Rose began life as Melba Christine Marcades on October 14, 1923 in Texas. The year of her birth has been disputed, with some reports or records listing "1922" and "1935" as the year of her birth.

However, one thing is certain. If the FBI arrest reports – which were from the U.S. Department of Justice dated October 23, 1964 – are to be believed, then Rose began her life of crime at the age of 17 with a charge of car theft. One of her earliest charges (under an alias of Patsy Sue Allen) was a charge of vagrancy at the age of 18 in San Antonio, Texas.

It would not be her final vagrancy charge or arrest. Rose, it seemed, began her life of crime with vagrancy and ended it as such.

Rose maintained that life of crime from February 13, 1941 to October 21, 1964 – with her final arrest being in New Orleans on a charge of investigated vagrancy and being "loud &

boisterous," according to the records. Her final arrest saw her listed as Roselle Renee Cherami.

Interestingly enough, Rose had allegedly told Lt. Francis Fruge and possibly others that she was in Eunice by way of Florida with the two men who resembled Italians, men who were to be the killers of JFK.

According to Fruge's testimony, Rose stated that she and the alleged killers left from Miami. But it was never revealed where exactly in Florida Rose had been either before or after the assassination of JFK.

However, it is her arrest record that sheds light on this matter.

Her second-to-last arrest (by sheriff's office officials) was listed on 6-12-64 in Titusville, Florida again under an alias, "Roselle." The name "Roselle" was used before by Rose, but this time developed further with the invention of "Roselle J. Crawford."

Oddly enough, the FBI records – which seemingly list Rose's charges in chronological order – showed a previous (third-to-last) charge as a more recent charge by the Pensacola Police Department of "drk" (drunkeness?) on 7-14-64 in Pensacola, Florida.

Using the name "Roselle Jeanne Cherami" in the Pensacola arrest, she had been arrested four months prior, again in Pensacola, on a similar charge. Clearly, Rose knew someone in Pensacola and seemed to make her way back and forth from Titusville – where, around the time of her Pensacola arrests, she was arrested again on 6-9-64. And then again about a week later in Cocoa Beach, Florida.

Rose obviously spent most of the summer in Florida, before returning to New Orleans for her final arrest on 10-19-64.

Was Cherami trying to state something for the record with the aliases used in her arrest reports?

The advent of the alias "Roselle" seemed curious and perhaps held clues that Rose tried to leave behind to anyone who might search for the truth, which Rose allegedly spoke and was paid no mind. Maybe out of frustration, because no one believed her about the JFK murder, she left coded clues in her aliases and arrest reports.

One curiosity with addresses, Rose was arrested in New Orleans (her final arrest) on 10-19-64 with her address listed as "757 Orion, Metairie, La."

However, just two days later, after she was photographed, fingerprinted and (presumably) released after time served for charges of drunken behavior and resisting arrest, Rose listed her address as "1004 Esplanade Avenue in New Orleans."

It should be noted that on this last arrest of her life, 10-19-64, in New Orleans, it was the first time that Rose was charged with resisting arrest.

The obvious "clue" of the alias "Roselle" pointed to Roselle, Illinois.

Roselle – which was a small village incorporated in 1922 – housed many commuters of nearby Chicago.

Was Rose pointing to Chicago?

Had she been there once and toyed with the name in her mind a time or two?

However, there is no record of Rose in Chicago or Illinois.

Chicago, of course, the home of Jack Ruby and a host of organized criminals like John "Handsome Johnny" Roselli.

Perhaps "Roselle" was a nod to Johnny Roselli – who was a high-ranking mob figure with ties to the CIA and the Chicago organized crime syndicate – the gangster who was found "whacked" and whose body was discovered decomposing in a steel drum near Miami in Dumbfounding Bay, Florida on August 9, 1976, around the time of the HSCA depositions and investigations.

Maybe Rose knew Roselli intimately and thus took the name Roselle as a link to a crime figure who would also ultimately be tied to JFK conspiracy chatter. Maybe Rose, an admitted drug trafficker, ran a little dope for Roselli now that Ruby was in prison.

The cities of Titusville and Cocoa Beach where Rose ran rampant are part of the Floridian "space coast," on the eastern side of the state. However, Pensacola is near the western-most edge of the state of Florida. These Florida arrests were of course after the JFK assassination.

Her arrests immediately before and after the JFK assassination are interesting.

Rose was arrested on 10-29-63 by the Houston Police Department for "drk & abu lang (drunk and abusive language)." Rose being in Houston at the time is significant because Sergio Arcacha-Smith (the Cuban man and CIA operative identified with Rose at the Silver Slipper) was allegedly living in Houston then.

When he was wanted by District Attorney Jim Garrison in 1967, Arcacha-Smith moved to Dallas. His extradition to Louisiana was purportedly blocked by Gov. John Connally himself.

Rose was next arrested on 12-28-63 by the Oklahoma City Police Department on a charge of "drk & (hold for state charges)," where she paid a $12-dollar fine and was released.

Curiously, however, the stay in the Eunice city jail (courtesy of the Eunice Police Department) is not in the FBI records. Nor is there any record of her transfer or commitment to the East Louisiana State Hospital from Eunice.

In fact, there are no arrests listed for Rose during the entire month of November 1963.

Perhaps the FBI would not bother with something as trivial as a transfer to a state hospital from a small town jail?

Yes, it would. The FBI certainly noted it in 1961.

Records reflected already that Rose had been interred in the Jackson East Louisiana State Hospital for being "criminally insane" in 1961. However, her second stay in the same hospital, the day before JFK's assassination, is not recorded by the FBI or Louisiana State Police.

According to documentation from the State of Louisiana Department of Public Safety, Division of State Police, Bureau of Investigation in Baton Rouge, Rose had been received by the Jackson East Louisiana State Hospital on 7-13-61. The charge: "Criminally Insane," according to Louisiana State Police record #256375 and FBI record #2-347-922.

It should be noted that the East Louisiana State Hospital in Jackson reportedly saw a number of physicians experimenting on prisoners with LSD and other hallucinogens.

If this hospital reception and charge was documented, why then was Rose's second stay at the state hospital omitted? By 1964, the FBI seemed to have forgotten to add her second stay in the state hospital to her permanent record. And would a visit to the drunk tank constitute a paper trail, adding to the blemishes on her criminal record?

Yes.

Rose was arrested several times in several different cities when she was charged with being drunk, often times being discharged after paying a fine the next day. However, the Eunice arrest, or stay in the drunk tank, was not in any of her criminal records.

Was it as Louis Pavur and Jane Carrier of Eunice said it was? Did "they" come and take all of the records of Rose's time in Eunice? Pavur's photocopy of an emergency room register at the Moosa hospital may be the only concrete evidence that Rose ever spent time in Eunice.

If she was not a person of interest, why then did the FBI have a record on Cherami dating back to 1941?

Furthermore, if Hoover and the Feds were aware of her criminal activity and aliases since 1941, why then did it seem that she was "permitted" to roam free? Curiously, Rose (after being charged with being criminally insane) had been put back out on the streets, loosed only to be arrested again a little more than two months later.

After being admitted into a state hospital and labeled as "criminally insane," it's hard to imagine that someone might be released less than 90 days later. But Rose was released.

And then arrested again. The Sheriff's Office in Gretna, Louisiana arrested a "Melba Marcades" on 9-22-61 on a charge of "vagrancy" shortly after her time as one of the "criminally insane" at the state hospital.

In fact, later in her criminal career, Rose was arrested by sheriff's officials in Altus, Oklahoma on a charge of "public drunkenness, suspect in narcotics and prostitution"; her only disposition stated that she was released "outright."

While labels such as "prostitute," "criminally insane" and "drug trafficker and addict" have been placed on Rose, one other label that should have easily been associated with Rose was "car thief." Some of her early 1941 arrests show a charge of "auto theft," and numerous arrests charge her with violation of the Dyer Act – the National Motor Vehicle Theft Act (18 U.S.C.A. § 2311 et seq.), signed into federal law in 1919 to impede the interstate trafficking of stolen vehicles by organized thieves.

Was Rose then an organized thief? Does this support evidence that Rose had a relationship with organized crime figures and families?

Rose, according to FBI records, had at least six charges and arrests for violation of the Dyer Act from 1947 to 1957 in Louisiana and New Mexico.

Rose told authorities that she was 17 when she was arrested for "car theft" in Amarillo, Texas in 1941. It was her first auto theft arrest, and a crime for which she served a little time in prison in Gainesville, Texas.

About a year later, the most curious charge of all for Rose Cherami came to light. While inventing aliases and dabbling in car theft was not the norm for a teen delinquent in 1941, her next charge reached a new level in her criminal career.

In 1942, while the country was at war, Rose was arrested in Shreveport, Louisiana (shortly after her release from a Texas prison) by the Sheriff's Office with a charge of "Hold for Barksdale" listed on her rap sheet of 9-30-42.

"Barksdale" referred to Barksdale airfield which had begun to gear up for WWII and which would be home to the oldest bomb wing division in the USAF as part of the Air Force Global Strike Command. Barksdale Air Force Base was branded, or renamed, on January 13, 1948, after the United States Air Force became a separate military branch.

But back in the mid-1930s it was home to the 3rd Bomber Wing of the U.S. military, and in the 1940s it hosted a number of bomber squadrons, notably the 335th Bombardment Group which took over training duties as a permanent Operational Training Unit (OTU) on July 17, 1942 with Martin B-26 Marauders.

Shortly after, Rose was charged with "aiding soldiers to escape" on September 30, 1942. By October 10, 1942, according to the arrest report, Rose was released to "USM"(United States Military?) on a charge of "aiding soldiers to escape."

At a most pivotal time in U.S. history, the seemingly egregious charge of "aiding soldiers to escape" might have been punishable by death, as Americans of Japanese descent were at the time being rounded up in "concentration camps" in the United States for merely being Japanese.

But what soldiers was Rose aiding to escape?

If Rose was "aiding soldiers to escape," then were they enemy soldiers (POWs) or U.S. soldiers? Her arrest record yields little details. According to the arrest report, Rose was released by the U.S. military with no disposition stated on the "aiding soldiers to escape" charge.

Nearly one month later, on 11-6-42, Rose was released to the custody of the state of Louisiana, where she was transferred to the Louisiana State Penitentiary, or Angola Prison, in West Feliciana Parish on 11-9-42 on a charge of "larceny."

It should be noted that Angola would be the future site of CIA-funded human, medical experimentation on prisoners for research into behavior modification during the 1950s.

After tangling with the U.S. military in her charge of "aiding soldiers to escape," less than two years later Rose was then released from Angola back into society on 10-9-44.

After being released in 1944, Rose seemed to "go straight," with no arrests until 1947 – when she would begin to rack up charges of auto-theft violations of the Dyer Act, for a total of six times in ten years.

And yet she continued her life of crime unhindered, undeterred by her criminal record. Only by the 1960s would the words "hold for state charges" begin to appear on her arrest records. Yet no law enforcement agency could seem to hold her for very long.

How was this possible?

In regards to those strangest of charges, from September 30, 1942 she was in the custody of the Sheriff's Department for "aiding soldiers to escape" from Barksdale. Then, by 10-10-42 she was released to the military. If she wasn't sent to Angola until 11-6-42, then where was Rose during that month?

What events transpired with the then-teenaged Rose while she was in the custody of the U.S. military for nearly one month? How did the charge of "aiding soldiers to escape" and her stint in prison seemingly get reduced to "larceny"?

Is it possible that she may have been "flipped" to work as an agent for the Office of Strategic Services (OSS), a precursor to the CIA formed during WWII? The OSS had just been officially signed into existence by the President of the United States, Franklin D. Roosevelt, some three months before Rose would be "aiding soldiers to escape."

The OSS, according to recently released personnel files, had more than 24,000 U.S. citizens in its employment (which included celebrity Julia Child under her maiden name) during WWII, according to the Central Intelligence Agency's official website.

The CIA described the OSS as an "unusual experiment – to determine whether a group of Americans constituting a cross section of racial origins, abilities, temperaments and talents could meet and risk an encounter with the long-established and well-trained enemy organizations."

However, near the time of the arrest and charge of "aiding soldiers to escape," Rose was also arrested under the name of "Mrs. Albert Rodman" of Shreveport, Louisiana.

Her relation to Albert Rodman is unknown.

Declassified OSS personnel files list one "Albert Rodman" – who was an immigrant from Russia who entered the port of Boston many years prior to the event.

The only declassified OSS personnel that resembled Rose (in name) was a "Lefty J. Cheramie," with little or no information regarding the agent.

Among the listed occupations in her arrest reports, it is documented that she was a waitress who lived in Sport, Louisiana to be held for Barksdale Field (now an Air Force base). After being held by the military for nearly a month, the now 20 year-old (who had a birthday while being detained) then listed her occupation as "stenographer" before being turned over to the state for her prison stint in Angola in Louisiana.

So, after a month of being held for by the U.S. military for "aiding soldiers to escape," somehow the waitress became a stenographer? Was she just lying or was she given some military or intelligence training? Why or how was it that she was arrested as a waitress, yet went to Angola a stenographer?

Rose was also an entertainer who lived at 824 Royal Street in New Orleans, a 33-year-old barmaid who lived at 222 South Gayoso Street in New Orleans and was arrested for arson (Rose's last recorded New Orleans address in 1964 was 1004 Esplanade Avenue) and, proven by an old photograph, she was a telephone operator in the mid to late 1950s.

Coupled with her new-found (military?) training as a stenographer, could her experience as a telephone operator have presented Rose with an opportunity to overhear a plot to assassinate JFK? Could she have been made an operative of the FBI or of the U.S. Department of Justice?

Curiously, the idea of Cherami working for the government was put forth in the collected testimony and published findings of the HSCA in April of 1979. According to the documents, after the Kennedy assassination, Rose (using the name Rozella Clinkscales) tipped FBI agents to prostitution rings; which were transporting women (as well as Rose herself) to cities like Galveston and Houston in Texas as well as Oklahoma City and Montgomery, Alabama.

It is further revealed in the HSCA findings that, in 1965, Rose tipped the FBI agents to a ship in New Orleans that was transporting a large amount of heroin into the country through the Port of New Orleans. FBI verified with a call to U.S. Coast Guard officials that indeed the ship was under a narcotics investigation at the time.

The FBI, after this tip from Rose, seemed to drop their pursuit in the matter of this information, though Rose could now be seen as an official informant for the FBI. According to the HSCA findings, "just 1 month after she contacted the FBI" about the prostitution and the drugs, Rose was found dead. It was also revealed in the HSCA report that the FBI had no knowledge that their informant had been found dead on September 4, 1965.

Louisiana State Police, according to the record, had no idea that the FBI had an interest in Rose when Lt. Fruge began in 1967 to investigate her "accidental death" on behalf of the District Attorney of Orleans Parish, Jim Garrison.

Garrison would have been very interested in Rose's State of Louisiana Department of Public Safety-Division of State Police records, which also state that on January 1, 1958 she was admitted as a patient to St. Elizabeths Hospital in Washington, D.C. – a mental hospital that could be nicknamed "the assassins hospital," as it housed the attempted presidential assassins Richard Lawrence (the would-be assassin of President Andrew Jackson) and John Hinckley, Jr. (famous for his assassination attempt on President Ronald Reagan). During his trial and while awaiting execution, St. Elizabeths also housed Charles J. Guiteau, who assassinated President James Garfield in 1881.

Prior to her St. Elizabeths stint, Rose was arrested in Albuquerque, New Mexico, for violating the Dyer Act. The next entry on her arrest record showed that she wound up in St. Elizabeths Hospital for possibly more than two years, as her next arrest showed her in Oklahoma City on 6-3-60.

Rose's stay in Washington, D.C. is significant because it was the same St. Elizabeths Hospital that purportedly saw the OSS testing "truth serums" on unwitting patients during WWII.

According to H.P. Albarelli's book *A Secret Order*, St. Elizabeths Hospital was the site of CIA "behavior modification" projects using CIA physicians. The CIA projects, like MK/ULTRA, reportedly tested LSD on mental patients, prisoners, drug addicts and prostitutes. Rose possessed the ideal traits for a CIA guinea pig, a person who could not fight back.

Her appearance in Oklahoma, confirmed by her arrest record, soon after her release from St. Elizabeths is also significant, as it is near another mental facility in Norman, Oklahoma – where the CIA began covertly operating their MK/ULTRA behavior modification or mind-control project at the Central State Mental Hospital, according to Albarelli's book.

As it turns out Rose was arrested three years later in Norman, Oklahoma, on 6-1-63.

Oddly enough, Lee Harvey Oswald had a Norman, Oklahoma address written down in his address book with no name attached to it, according to Albarelli – who alleges that Rose was a patient in that Norman, Oklahoma facility. The HSCA report says the FBI claimed that Rose had been "confined" to a mental institution in Norman on three separate occasions.

But, in regards to St. Elizabeths, how did Rose get admitted to a massive, federally funded, government-operated Washington, D.C. mental hospital following an arrest in New Mexico? If she went to the District of Columbia on her own accord, then what business did she have in D.C. to begin with? There is no record of Rose spending any other time in D.C.

Interestingly enough, in 2007, the old St. Elizabeths Hospital became the new home of the Department of Homeland Security.

On his second birthday, Michael Marcades with his mother in Houston, Texas, February 13, 1955.
Photo courtesy of Dr. Michael Marcades.

Chapter Nine

Young Blood

During Jim Garrison's investigation into the possible plot to kill JFK, Garrison compiled a box of information on Rose. The more than 40 pages of Garrison's files, which Garrison's son donated to the National Archives in Washington, D.C. shed more light on Rose.

Another name keeps circling around the JFK conspiracy and Rose Cherami: Youngblood. Perhaps a married name, Rose used the last name Youngblood on more than one occasion.

According to the FBI files, Rose was arrested in Amarillo, Texas under the name of Christine Youngblood on 6-12-41 for car theft. She was released to Dallas Sheriff's Office authorities on other charges of car theft. She was incarcerated at the Gainesville reformatory prison in Texas on 6-15-41.

After being released from Gainesville, she was arrested again in Shreveport, Louisiana under the name "Melba Christine Youngblood" on an investigation charge for larceny dated back to 8-7-42.

However, again we see Rose as "Melba Christine Youngblood Rodman," this time on 9-30-42, when her charge stated "hold for Barksdale."

The infamous, "aiding soldiers to escape" charge happened on 10-10-42 to Melba Christian Youngblood Rodman.

By 1947, in New Orleans, after her time in Angola prison, she was arrested under the name Melba Christine Youngblood for disturbing the peace in a police station by using obscene language. New Orleans police added to her charge these words: "subject believed to be insane."

When the charge came up before the powers that be, prosecution was declined and the complaint was dismissed. Perhaps the name Youngblood carried some weight with it in certain circles of New Orleans at the time.

Her later criminal record also points to a possible date that she could have worked in Jack Ruby's Carousel Club in Dallas.

Rose was arrested in Dallas for being drunk and disorderly, this time under her real name of Melba Christine Marcades, on 5-15-63 – which was little more than six months prior to Kennedy's murder in that city.

Was this when she overheard something about a plot to kill JFK?

By the 1950's, according to her criminal record, Rose ceased using the last name Youngblood. It's possible that it was a married name, rather than an assumed name.

In Garrison's file, companioned with Rose's arrest records and various notes, is a weighty section of FBI files of a man named Robert George Youngblood. According to FBI file of record number "222-651-A," Robert George Youngblood has listed as a contributor of his fingerprints, "Army." The date of 7-13-40 is listed as his date of being arrested or received in Houston, Texas.

Then again on 8-21-42, the contributor of fingerprints listed "CAA, Wash., D.C." also with the words "applicant F.P." on the documentation that was once in the hands of Jim Garrison. This was about one month prior to Rose being arrested for "aiding soldiers to escape" at Barksdale Airfield.

This Robert George Youngblood was also arrested in Reno on the charge of being a "shill" on 12-10-46.

By 1949, Youngblood was released into the custody of the USM (United States Military) in New Orleans where he was "on Gov. Reservation," after he was arrested on 6-30-49 on a charge of theft of government property. According to the file, the charge was pending.

At first glance, the charge of "theft of government property" reeks of gun running. Gun runners back then (and possibly still today) were often military or ex-military who would steal weapons from military installations, or as stated in the file, a "government reservation."

There are similarities between his crime record and that of Rose.

He was a known car thief with a list of aliases that included Johnnie C. Youngblood, Johnnie Cleveland Youngblood, J.C. Gaines, Jake Youngblood and J.C. Youngblood. The Atlanta Police Department arrested Jake Youngblood for being a suspect in an "assault to murder charge" on 5-8-48.

However, by 1950 the information on Youngblood goes "dark," with his final arrest on 1-6-50, in Atlanta, for violation of the Dyer Act, much like Rose. According to the paperwork, his disposition is "pending" with no release to a prison or any further arrests.

Curiously enough, the last name Youngblood breathed new life with a mention in the Warren Commission Report, from the sworn testimony of a woman with New Orleans connections.

Nancy Perrin Rich, who was mentioned in a hand written note in Garrison's files with the inscribed message: "man by this name was at party – Nancy Perrin Rich." The writing had a arrow drawn on the page pointing to the name "Youngblood" as it pertained to Melba Christine Youngblood: Rose.

The testimony of Nancy Perrin Rich was taken at 11 A.M., on June 2, 1964, at 200 Maryland Avenue NE., Washington, D.C., by Burt W. Griffin and Leon D. Hubert, Jr., assistant counsel of the Warren Commission. In her testimony, Rich described how at the time of the testimony she resided in Massachusetts and how her previous husband, Robert L. Perrin, died in New Orleans in 1962 by arsenic poisoning, which was ruled a suicide.

She mentioned how her late husband once worked for a man named Jack Dragna, who, at the time, was serving time in San Quentin prison. Dragna and his associates were members of organized crime, and her husband was as well.

She claimed that her husband ran guns to General Franco in Spain during the war and that his new Mafia associates were about "everything from prostitution to illegal gambling to narcotics." She also said that her husband served time in a Spanish prison, that he was "a professional soldier" who fought for both sides.

Rich claimed that while the couple did reside for a time in Belmont, Massachusetts, her husband left her while he made his way to Dallas, Texas.

Seeking him out, she began to call Dallas looking for her husband to rejoin him, according to her testimony in the Warren Commission Report:

"Mrs. RICH. I was in New Hampshire with the state legislature at the time. I was doing public relations. And I had just obtained a job, a position for him, and I telephoned to Massachusetts to tell him to come on down, and there was no answer. And I had a feeling that something was wrong. So I hightailed it back to Massachusetts, and there was a note. And the note said that he was going to Dallas. I called and he wasn't there. I called halfway over the United States, thinking of places he told me he had been, and I couldn't find him.

"Mr. HUBERT. What place did you call in Dallas?

"Mrs. RICH. I called the police department and a foundry he had mentioned in a letter, and had read the name of a gentleman he had mentioned at this time whose name eludes me – Youngblood – I take it back.

"Mr. HUBERT. Do you remember his first name?

"Mrs. RICH. No; I don't. But my husband claimed – and I couldn't ask him, because if he was he couldn't have told me – claimed he was some sort of a Government agent, which was in all probability true.

"Mr. HUBERT. Did you contact Mr. Youngblood?

"Mrs. RICH. Yes; he hadn't seen him. Then I proceeded to call Kansas City and various other points I thought he might be."

Thus, according to the Warren Commission, in 1961 Youngblood was the name of a mysterious "government agent" living in Dallas, who knew a Mafia-connected, mercenary named

Robert L. Perrin, who wound up dead in about a year's time in New Orleans.

According to Mrs. Rich's testimony, one of the first people that she met when she arrived in Dallas was officer J.D. Tippit – who was also slain in Dallas on November 22, 1963. Mrs. Rich said that she had spoken to Tippit by phone over a period of time before leaving for Dallas.

Allegedly, Tippit, or others at the Dallas Police Department, helped her to establish a residence at a boarding house until she could find her husband.

Her first job while in Dallas was at Jack Ruby's Carousel Club as a bartender. Nancy Perrin Rich just rolled into town from Massachusetts and happened to meet two major characters in the JFK mystery, possibly because of her connections with her husband and this "Youngblood" agent.

In Garrison's notes, the "party" that Mrs. Rich attended was actually a series of three meetings in a scantly furnished apartment in Dallas.

Her husband's friend in Dallas, one David Cherry (which sounds a lot like David Ferrie), helped to broker a deal to do some work that needed the precision and discipline of a mercenary.

Mrs. Rich claimed that they met with a Colonel or possibly a Lt. Colonel of the U.S. Army in the bare apartment in Dallas. The Colonel offered her husband $10,000 to help pilot a boat to Cuba in an effort to help Cuban refugees to escape while also running rifles into mainland Cuba.

According to Garrison's research, Youngblood attended at least one of the meetings.

Mrs. Rich claimed that at the second meeting, Jack Ruby showed up with a bulge in his coat pocket. She claimed that she assumed Ruby brought a large amount of cash to the party, because everybody was happy to see Jack.

She said Ruby glared at her in disbelief or shock, because she and her husband used aliases that night. Ruby knew her real name, but played along and left abruptly.

When she counter-offered $25,000 for the job of piloting and gun-running a boat to Cuba, the colonel offered $15,000 at the third meeting, which was also attended by a new face that Mrs. Rich believed to be, according to her testimony, the son of a powerful mob figure.

They fled that apartment for the last time, not taking the job or the money. She implied that she and her husband packed their things that night, or shortly thereafter, and drove to New Orleans. About a year later, her husband would be dead, but not before "turning her out" as a prostitute.

Years later, the name of Youngblood would come up once again in the investigation of another assassination, named by James Earl Ray, the charged and convicted (but never confessed) assassin of Martin Luther King, Jr., during a filmed interview for the HSCA MLK Report (vol.1 p.242) during the 1970s investigations.

In his sworn testimony, Ray said that an FBI agent came to visit him while in prison in 1969 to seek his help in regards to taking "some people out of circulation." He claimed that the agent showed him about 10 to 15 "pictures that the FBI wanted taken out of circulation" of Latin-looking individuals and even some pictures taken from Dealey Plaza in 1963 immediately following the shooting.

"One picture was taken in Dallas or something, in 1963," said Ray in his sworn testimony for the HSCA. "There was no names given. And one picture was an individual named Jack Youngblood."

Youngblood would be known to most MLK conspiracy theorists as the "eggs and sausages man," a stranger who was seen frequenting the nearby diner within days of and the day of the assassination. Youngblood was allegedly arrested immediately after the MLK shooting, but was never held.

In Waldron's *Legacy of Secrecy*, it is stated that James Earl Ray was much like Rose, in the sense that they were both drug couriers operating for the same Marcello heroin network.

On Rose Cherami's death certificate, the name of Thomas J. Youngblood was listed as her father's name and as the deceased's informant.

Was this Jack Youngblood any relation to Rose? If her father's name was Youngblood, could it have been a brother rather than a husband?

With her mother's name listed on the death certificate as Minnie Stroud, Rose must have had some sense of humor in choosing her aliases: she also went by "Mickey," possibly to her mother's "Minnie."

But how does a father named Youngblood and a mother named Stroud add up to a daughter name Melba Christine Marcades?

While there were other underworld rumblings of foreknowledge of JFK's possible assassination becoming inevitable or discussed by the likes of Joseph Milteer – who was a Florida right-wing militant who loathed JFK for his liberal policies – Rose was the first to give an exact time and place: Dallas, Texas on Friday, November 22, 1963.

While some contend that Rose "laid with dogs and got fleas" as an explanation for her foreknowledge, the possibility of Rose appearing as more of a government agent, or in some way connected to characters in both the criminal underworld and a government agency becomes more plausible.

If Rose was just a prostitute or whore (the common whore would have been relegated to the whore houses along the

The man known as Jack Youngblood, also known as the "eggs and sausages man" for his possible involvement in the assassination of Martin Luther King.

Allegedly he was arrested shortly after the MLK slaying but was released. A waitress, in a neighborhood cafe near the MLK's assassination site, thought he was a suspicious person. Being a stranger, the waitress only knew him by his breakfast order of eggs and sausages.

Photo courtesy of the HSCA mugbook and maryferrell.org

wooded highways of Louisiana), she would never have been permitted to be in on any conversation, in some inner circle, where the business of the president's murder was being discussed.

While she dealt in prostitution and drugs, it would also appear that she dealt in information. Rose seemed to make it her business to know where and when large shipments of heroin would enter the country and where young girls were being sold into the sex trade. More importantly, she shared her information with authorities.

Many people were associated with the underworld at the time, yet hardly anyone heard specifically that JFK would be murdered on a Friday in Dallas.

If they did, they kept quiet.

Rose did not.

It looked as if Rose "positioned" herself to be in the right place, at the right time. In other words, she caught the right fleas, lying with the right dogs at the right time.

Chapter Ten

The Long D.O.A. of Rose Cherami

J ust as her life was shrouded in mystery, so was her death. It seems that Rose left the surreal in her wake.

On September 4, 1965, as Jack Ruby sat in a Dallas prison cell for the murder of Oswald, Cherami was again hit by a car, or at least found on the side of a highway.

This time the injuries proved fatal.

Her death certificate read that she was found dead outside of Gladewater, Texas, apparently after she had been walking on Highway 155 about one and a half miles east of Big Sandy at about 2 A.M.

In fact, when she was found, she was still alive and breathing.

According to some accounts, at 2:15 A.M., Jerry Don Moore of Tyler, Texas was driving out of Big Sandy down a stretch of Highway 155 he had also driven down 15 minutes earlier. He saw something strange in the road that hadn't been there 15 minutes before. Moore recalls seeing three or four suitcases laid along the yellow line in the middle of the road. He swerved to the right to miss the luggage. That was when he noticed the woman lying on the side of the road.

All of this was verified by Moore, himself, in a published 2010 interview for *Lagniappe Magazine*, a bi-weekly, free tabloid based in Lake Charles, Louisiana.

"It looked like she was sleeping," Moore recalled. "She had her arms folded under her head like she was sleeping, with her elbows out. She was laid out parallel to the highway on the right-hand side, and she wasn't in the road; maybe her elbow was, but it was just barely in the road. She was more in the gravel between the highway to her left and the grass and the ditch to her right."

Reacting quickly so as not to hit this person on the side of the highway, Moore said that he slammed on his brakes, which "banged" under his car's chassis twice as he swerved.

"I know I didn't hit her. I ran off into the ditch and finally got my car up out of the ditch and back onto the road. And then I went to check on her and she was still breathing, but very short breaths – and then she would stop. And that's when I noticed tread marks on her arms. But the car I drove then had bald tires with no treads. It looked like someone else had run over her."

Moore was asked whether he thought the mysteriously positioned pieces of luggage in the middle of the highway were strategically placed with the intention of forcing a motorist to swerve and hit the laid-out Cherami.

"Hell yeah, as night is night and day is day, you could tell it was a set-up to run over that woman," said Moore. "It looked as if someone had done this sort of thing before."

Moore admitted to doing 70 to 80 miles per hour and drinking his libation of choice, Seagram's Seven Crown, all night. He also admitted to trying to assist a barely alive Rose Cherami. He claimed he stopped a car of black men and women traveling north on the highway. But they didn't seem anxious to help move the suitcases out of the road as he asked them to. He claimed that at this point, he noticed a red Chevrolet parked on the side of the road opposite of the spot where he'd found Cherami. He figured it was a 1963 or 1964 model, a relatively new car.

"It was in the roadside park area. It was cherry red. The lights were off and the engine was off," said Moore. "I couldn't see anyone in the vehicle."

Moore wondered if there was someone in that car, waiting. Could someone have been in that car watching this scene unfold in the darkness? Did someone need to verify that a loose end like Rose had been knotted up?

After Moore grabbed Cherami under her arms and loaded her body into his back seat, Moore said, he then drove her into town for medical attention.

He stopped briefly in Hawkins, Texas, where he was told by a policeman that the nearest hospital was in Gladewater. But the police officer knew of a doctor in Hawkins and offered Moore a police escort.

On her arrival at the doctor's home, Cherami was laid out in the early morning dew of a front yard. After a quick examination, the doctor phoned an ambulance and had Cherami taken to Gladewater Memorial Hospital. Moore recalled the doctor giving her a couple of shots and telling him she was suffering from brain damage.

"I was concerned." said Moore. "I was scared. And I didn't hit her. Nor did I expect any of this. I really just wanted to get home to Tyler that night."

But he didn't drive back to Tyler immediately. He waited until the ambulance came and followed it to the hospital. After that, he returned to the site of her luggage still mysteriously placed on the yellow highway line on 155.

"I thought I could help identify her. So I went and got her luggage for her. I did go through some of her luggage to look for a name or an ID. But then I brought her luggage back to the hospital."

Curiously, Moore said that he figured that she was a whore because of the fact that he found a "douche-bag" or "hot water bottle" in one of her suitcases. He explained that it was a tell-tale sign of a prostitute.

It's alleged that at some point, Cherami remarked to one of the ambulance crew or hospital staff, "I worked for Jack Ruby." Perhaps Rose thought that was important enough that people should know about it unto her last breath.

None of these allegations have ever been verified with members of the hospital staff.

However, one thing was certain, Cherami faded into the blackness of death less than two years after JFK was murdered.

As the morning faded into place, Moore finally got home to Tyler at 4:30 A.M. Energized from the strange set of circumstances, he couldn't sleep.

Worried, concerned and possibly feeling guilty, he soon found himself back at the Gladewater Memorial Hospital – between 9:30 and 10 A.M. – to check on Cherami.

As Moore returned to the hospital, his strange morning got a bit stranger. The woman he found had died. Hospital staff informed him they had called in a doctor from Dallas who came in the wee hours of morning.

"I surely didn't think that she would die," said Moore. "I mean, she didn't seem to be in that bad of a condition. There wasn't a single drop of blood on my car, on her, or in my backseat. I didn't see any blood. They told me 'after that Dallas doctor got here, she didn't last long.'"

Why would a fully functional hospital call for a doctor in Dallas, which is 80 miles away? And who was this Dallas doctor?

In three places on her death certificate are the letters D.O.A. (denoting "dead on arrival"). Yet the certificate states the time of death was 11 A.M. The time of the accident is clearly marked 2 A.M. on the death certificate.

This begs the question, did it take nine hours for Rose Cherami to die? How long did it take to get to the nearest hospital — seven hours?

Even if Rose had been driven to a Dallas hospital to be pronounced DOA, the certificate would have recorded an earlier time of death than 11 A.M.

"I know I was there by 10 A.M. and they said she was already dead," said Moore. "So I don't know where they got that 11 A.M. I thought they told me that she died around 7:30 that morning."

Investigations were open and shut rather quickly. Moore claimed that the day after Cherami's death, the Highway Patrol showed up at his door to investigate his vehicle. They found no blood on the exterior of Moore's vehicle, not a drop of blood in the back seat, and nothing to directly link Cherami and Moore. The case seemed closed.

"When they came over the next morning, I thought it was strange that they seized my driver's license. I don't know why they took my license. They didn't even give me a ticket. They held on to my license for six months."

When Moore was asked why he thought that they did this, he replied, "Beats the shit out of me."

Some suggest that when she was found, Cherami had a small caliber bullet lodged in her skull. The death certificate didn't mention a bullet, just damage to her skull.

Where was Rose going?

Why were her bags taken out to the middle of the road and seemed to be strategically placed there?

Whom was she riding with?

Did she know the person?

Was this just another unfortunate accident for Rose Cherami?

Over the years, Moore would hear urban legends about Cherami, the woman whose fate had become entwined with his own. The most interesting story Moore told was that she had been driven to Texas from New Orleans on the night before she was found on the road.

According to Moore, legend has it that she got in a car with "some Navy boys" from New Orleans and they were bound for Dallas that night. Supposedly, they took a wrong turn off Highway 80 towards Big Sandy. This would have put them on Highway 155 at sometime early the next morning. As the story screeches to a halt, there's little explanation as to whether these men had paid her to have sex or had raped her and refused to pay her and had then kicked her out of their vehicle.

Was it coincidence or an amalgamation with the Highway 190-Eunice story?

The newspaper that reported on her death gave Rose another alias: "a Duncanville woman" who was found dead.

Rose's death certificate listed her address as Duncanville, Texas. The area where Rose was found near Big Sandy, Texas, is hell and gone, more than 100 miles away from Duncanville, Texas. Rose was found on a farm-to-market road – which would have been a poor choice for any hitchhiker, as it was in between two major highways.

The newspaper that reported her death, the *Gladewater Mirror*, played Rose's death as a front-page, statistical news story about how dangerous the highway was, as it had claimed another life. The paper made no mention of her real story, her family or her possible connection with the JFK assassination.

Even the death certificate, itself, makes odd Rose's end at the age of 41.

The time of injury is listed at "2:00 A.M." In the space on the death certificate which denoted the interval between onset and death, the record shows: "8 hrs."

The coroner in Gladewater filled in the three blanks on the certificate with "D.O.A.," three times in places that concerned statistical date information.

In other words, her death certificate would read: "I hereby certify that I attended the deceased from D.O.A., 19___ to D.O.A., 19___ and last saw the deceased alive on D.O.A., 19___."

Did the coroner overstate the obvious? Does any coroner certify living persons?

Ross Delay, the coroner in Gladewater in 1965, signed off on Rose's death certificate on 9-11-65, five days after her body had already been removed for burial by funeral home personnel.

Rogers Funeral Home, under the direction of Rex F. Rogers, assisted in burying the truth in the Wheatland Cemetery in Texas.

Before being a subject of myths, Cherami was the subject of an autopsy, which the Texas hospital was unable to locate in 1967 when Jim Garrison hired investigators to get the report. To this day, no investigator has seen the autopsy report on Cherami.

The man who may have the only existing copy of the autopsy report, possibly one of the few persons to have viewed the report, is Rose's son, Michael.

Chapter Eleven

Son of Rose Cherami

A s Lt. Francis Fruge and many others believed that Rose Cherami had direct knowledge of the assassination plot, so does her son.

Dr. Michael Marcades, 60, the Director of Music Ministries of First Methodist Church in Opelika, Alabama, had a minor role in the strange tale of Rose Cherami as "her baby." If there can be a real biography of Rose Cherami, only one man could truly complete every chapter from his perspective.

He said that he was 10 at time of the JFK assassination.

"My mother may have been a lot of things, but she wasn't a liar," said Marcades in a 2012 phone interview for the *Eunice News*. "When it came down to life and death, in her mind I think she knew the difference between right and wrong. Was she a prostitute? Yes. Was she a drug trafficker? Yes. Did she lose her entire sense of moral compass? No.

"I don't believe that she was lying. I believe that she told the truth out of frustration. I believe in that hospital in Louisiana, she was screaming the truth and no one would listen because of her background. I mean, how different life and history would have been had someone actually paid attention to the ravings of a prostitute-drug trafficker."

Marcades said that he, like many others, believes that she is the first JFK assassination conspiracy theorist. He noted that she believed in a conspiracy while President Kennedy was still alive.

In a 2013 interview, Marcades questioned some of the state records which deemed his mother "criminally insane." "What did criminally insane mean in 1961? Was it that she was a

The son of Rose Cherami, Dr. Michael Marcades, in 2013.
Photo by Todd C. Elliott

woman who had a tendency to be involved in criminal activity? And that was deemed criminally insane?

"The things that I remember about her: she was beautiful, well kept. She was brilliant. She was capable of learning and doing just about anything."

At the time of Rose's death, Marcades stated that he was living with his grandparents in the Houston area or had possibly then just recently moved to the Dallas area.

He said that he does remember living in Houston up until the 4th grade. "I was probably in Richardson, Texas," he said, during Rose's final days.

Marcades said that he agreed with the St. Landry Parish Assistant Coroner, Dr. DeRouen – who in 1963 allegedly determined that Rose had been a heroin addict for 7 to 9 years in the days leading up to the assassination.

"Somewhere around 1957 or 1958, saw her periodically, after that just a few more times ... but I remember them well.

Marcades said. "I want you to understand that I don't walk on eggshells about my mother. I have a great deal of pride. I believe my mother was a brilliant individual who got off on the wrong track and didn't know how to recover. And she had some tendencies in her personality that kept her from returning, possibly, to what we would refer to a normal life. And then at some point there was probably no option to return."

At times during the interview, Marcades would refer to "Melba" as his mother and at other times as "Rose" or "Rose Cherami," possibly very much like his mother did.

"Rose Cherami was just a name that was used near the ending of her life," he said. Marcades said that he did not know where the alias of "Rose Cherami" derived from.

"Although I think that she used different names in different locations for different functions as everyone near her did," he said. "I don't know where that name came from. I can look at some of the names and deduce where they originated, but not 'Rose Cherami'. I have no clue.

"I know this woman from many different perspectives. When you mention Melba Christine Marcades, or Melba Christine Youngblood Marcades, that's the woman that I know as my mother," said Marcades. "All these other names are different aspects of a human that I have spent 30 years trying to understand and discover ... without a lot of help."

Michael said that he remembered living in the New Orleans area, when he was very young.

And when he was older, he also searched and sought out clues to solving the mystery of his mother, possibly in hopes of gaining some closure. He recalled the arduous task of getting her medical records from the Gladewater Hospital, the place where he said his mother breathed her last breath.

"It was an unusual process [in 1983]. Nothing that I experienced on site was what I would label as normal," he said. "It took me hours to get access to what I should have been able to have access to in 15 minutes. After hours of the hospital staff frantically searching and making a phone call or two, the file was then pulled out from a very illogical location, it wasn't in a drawer where you pull out a file drawer and look under the 'M's'. It was oddly misplaced, oddly located and oddly presented."

Marcades said that he recalled the first time that he saw his mother, "notoriously preserved" in the *JFK* film portrayal. "If there's one thing that Oliver Stone depicted accurately, it's my mother's frustration to be believed," he said. "There was no foundation for her to be believed."

He said that Stone's shot of Rose Cherami's highway death scene, complete with aligned luggage in the background, was a perfect depiction of what the details surrounding her mysterious death suggest.

"Learning her truth, learning as much truth as I can uncover, is 'freeing' for me," he said. "I'm aware of lots of levels of sacrifices on her part toward me as her son. In the midst of all of this, what you see or what the public sees has nothing to do with what I see as her son, and her sacrificial actions of a mother protecting a son.

"I know there were times when Mother would not communicate with me directly for years," he said. "But yet, she communicated with others about me. And in her effort to protect me she would never come directly to me. Perhaps she observed me from across the street at a playground.

"But I think that there were probably times, given where she was in her life, that if she were going to see me, I would be unaware of it."

When asked about his mother's tendency to, seemingly, skirt prosecution upon being arrested repeatedly, he commented.

"If something of that magnitude is occurring over and over … I would only say that someone had connections," he said.

When asked why he thought that his mother said anything about the JFK assassination, or why she would volunteer any information knowing that it would seal her fate, he answered:

"I think that it's the heart of who she was. If you look at [her criminal records] you won't discover her character," Marcades said. "Who she was from her upbringing even into her early teenage years, the essence, the values, the desire for truth, the difference between right and wrong ... although her life is full of what we would label as 'wrong', I'm sure that in her wrongness there were right acts laced in there. I'm convinced that there were times when she took care of people, when she overlooked something, when she lied to protect someone, myself included, or anyone else in our family. So in the final analysis ...

"I am a Christian, but I'm not a raving fundamentalist. And If I'm dying, on my deathbed, and I really come to the realization that things that I have heard all of my lifetime were true, then I seek resolution in whatever way it deems appropriate with God. That's what I see happening to my mother in these last days, of her knowing and the importance of what she knew. And the importance of trying to right it as much as she possibly could.

"Dead ends were the plan – by those who saw to it that her life was cut short," he said. "Many of those who knew her are dead. And those who are alive have different goals; some wish to forget, even without the entire truth. I don't fall into that category."

And what does the future hold for the son of Rose Cherami?

"Someone asked me recently, 'aren't you worried about this? Aren't you worried about continuing to ask questions? Aren't you scared?'

"Why should I be scared? Why should I be scared about seeking the truth, about the woman who gave birth to me," he said. "If something happens to me, there's too many people that know me. You know, it might be a real benefit for something to happen to me. It might actually foster truth. Because hundreds of people know me, many of them are discovering that I am the son of Rose Cherami."

At the time of this interview, Michael was in the process of writing his own book about his mother.

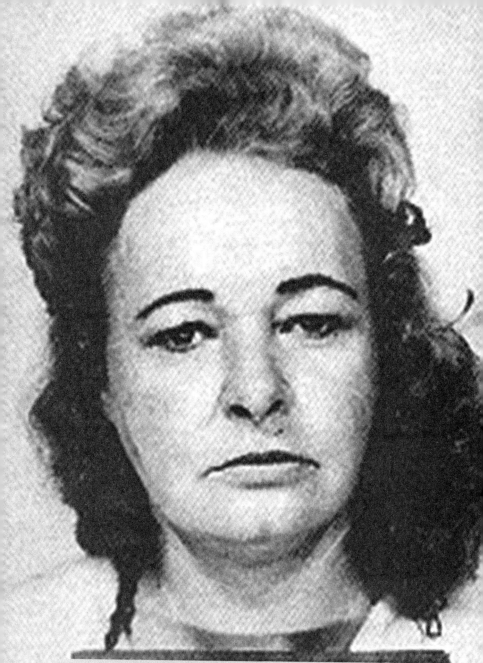

This is how most of the world, for years, has seen Rose Cherami. It is possibly one of the last photos taken of her. This is a mug shot from her arrest on October 19, 1964 for an investigation into vagrancy, being drunk and disturbing the peace. Curiously, two arrest reports were filed by State Police: one charge is "Resisting Arrest" by arresting officer G. Jones and the other is a charge of "Drunk, disturbing the peace" by arresting officer T. Calamia. Both arrest reports place the scene of the crime at U.S. 90 in St. Tammany Parish. Even stranger, her age is unknown and height 5'6" and weight 140, but in the second report this info regarding height and weight is unknown. Less than a year later, she would be dead.
Her son Michael said of this mugshot, "There is nothing behind those eyes."

First Person, Last Words

Rose Cherami was the strangest woman that I've never known.

A couple of strange incidents happened to me while I was writing this book, one of which, I will share.

First, let me state that for years I had always wanted to read a book on Rose Cherami. I had no idea, however, that I would be the one to write that book, the first book on Rose Cherami. After watching *JFK* for perhaps the 30th time, I decided to do an investigative journalist piece on something that I could research in my Louisiana backyard.

I had never been to Eunice, Louisiana until the summer of 2010. I was living in Lake Charles, some 50 miles away, at the time, while my wife was serving with the Louisiana National Guard deployed in Iraq.

Since Eunice is featured at the start of that film, I figured that it was a good place to start. I lucked out and found some individuals on day one who were still alive and remembered the legend of Rose Cherami.

When you follow history and the JFK conspiracy theories, you learn about all kinds of characters like Lee Harvey Oswald and Jack Ruby. And when I first rolled into town, I saw a place called Ruby's cafe, and that, jokingly, raised my eyebrow in my conspiratorial view of things.

Unfortunately, some people that I interviewed were (and still are) reluctant to go on the record, out of fear.

I felt that, in the face of this ingrained fear, I was doing the right thing. And I wanted to be first kid on my block to carry on the torch of truth seekers and researchers for a new generation for JFK, MLK and RFK researchers.

By the end of 2012, I secured gainful employment at the *Eunice News*. I wanted to work in Eunice, to develop, and hopefully solve, the mystery of Rose Cherami in the town that first heard her words.

On November 22, 2012, the 49th anniversary of the JFK assassination, my story on Rose Cherami made the front page of the *Eunice News*. I felt like it was a poetic justice in some way, and it was a surreal moment for me when I saw the printed edition.

The story ran in some of our sister newspapers and was featured on their respective websites.

The story was hot.

I had garnered more than 20,000 reads, or "page views," of my story on Rose, as it went viral in six days' time from the paper's eunicetoday.com website. At the time of this writing, the story had garnered over 26,000 views in about three months.

It was the biggest story of my career. Then the book deal came.

Then a strange, anonymous package came for me one day.

I was reading a story from a past-edition of the *Crowley Post Signal* – a sister paper to the *Eunice News* – which featured a guest writer who remembered when JFK visited Crowley, some 20 miles to the south of Eunice, in 1959 as a Senator with his lovely wife. The writer recalled how Jacqueline Kennedy spoke her Parisian French to the mostly Cajun-French crowd – who ate it up.

A contributor to the piece claimed that Crowley was "the birthplace of Camelot," due to the fact that shortly after JFK's visit to Crowley, he would announce his candidacy for President of the United States.

As I had written in my piece (and in this book) that Eunice, the next major town to the north, was "the birthplace of the JFK assassination conspiracy theory," I thought to myself, "How odd": it all began and ended in my neck of the woods.

Just after I finished reading the Crowley piece, one Friday in January 2013, I was told that a package had come for me. The package was anonymous, no return address. When I opened the package, I noticed that it was a box full of old, near-mint condition newspapers and magazines.

The final edition of the *Amarillo Globe-Times* for November 22, 1963 had a headline that read: "HIDDEN ASSASSIN KILLS PRESIDENT."

I always found the Associated Press story fascinating, as it ran all over the country stating that Dallas Police "believed that the fatal shots were fired by a white man about 30, slender of build, weighing about 165 pounds, and standing 5 feet 10 inches tall."

Even with today's technology, Dallas Police would be hard pressed to have that kind of a description for a murder suspect some 30 minutes following the murder. I often wondered why the Dallas Police didn't just put Oswald's address out there as well.

There were a couple of things on the front page of the now antique newspaper that I had never heard reported. Story headers at the bottom of the page read: " Young Man Is Arrested" and "Officer and Agent Slain."

The first story, also an AP story, read, "Soon after President Kennedy was assassinated today in Dallas, a white man in his mid 20s was arrested in the Riverside section Fort Worth in the shooting of a Dallas policeman."

Certainly this story was about the shooting of Dallas Police Officer J.D. Tippit. Many eyewitnesses never fingered Oswald for that murder and many researchers believed that Oswald could not have done the shooting, based on the ballistics and the timeline of the event.

The article stated that the man who was arrested had black, curly hair, unlike Oswald. I immediately thought of Jack Youngblood, who also had wavy, black hair.

The mystery man in the article was handcuffed and taken to Fort Worth city jail.

The second story on the front page stated that a Secret Service agent and a Dallas policemen were "shot and killed some distance from the area where President Kennedy was assassinated."

People well versed in the JFK conspiracy lore know of the aforementioned Dallas police officer slaying as that of J.D. Tippit. But this was the first that I'd ever heard about a Secret Service agent being slain.

Also included in the package was an edition of the *Springfield Daily News* for Friday, August 12, 1949.

Among big articles about U.S. military equipment being used to fight communists in Greece on August 11, 1949, I spotted a small story out of Miami with a curious headline: "Strip Tease Dancers Spend Night in Jail."

I immediately thought of Rose. And then, I thought, "Why would a Missouri newspaper run a story from Miami?"

According to the vintage news story, eight strippers were arrested in a nightclub in Dade County. The sheriff was quoted as saying, "We're cleaning up the county." I wondered how that had worked out for them down there in 1949.

Then there was an edition of the *Honolulu Advertiser* (Sunday) for March 16, 1952 included in my package.

The headline plastered atop the page read: "REDS PUSH 'GERM' CHARGE." A smaller headline near the top of the page read: "Propaganda Radio Blasts Stepped Up."

At the time, the Korean War was in full swing and the Red Chinese had allegedly begun a "germ warfare" campaign against the U.S. In the article, the Chinese accused the U.S. of dropping "germ-laden insects" from American planes. The Chinese claimed to have photographed "various types of containers" which contained fleas, mosquitoes and flies that had been dropped into communist territory by American forces.

I immediately thought of Judyth Vary Baker's book *Me & Lee*, and her research into a military-intelligence project which involved biological warfare. There were also echoes of *Dr. Mary's Monkey*, which also sheds light on biological warfare research.

However, below that story about U.S. germ warfare, another headline read: "U.S. Considers UN Probe Of Germ Claim." It was a one-paragraph story denouncing Soviet charges that the U.S. would engage in such a thing.

Mixed in with the old newspapers were 1963 issues of *Newsweek, Time* and *Life* magazines, which depicted JFK, LBJ and Secretary of State Dean Rusk on the covers.

Rusk, who was JFK's Secretary of State and carried over into the Johnson administration – was a man that JFK was disappointed with over the Bay of Pigs failure.

I also learned that Oswald, while he was in Russia as a defector, wrote to John Connally – who was the recently resigned Secretary of the U.S. Navy before he was the governor of Texas and shot alongside JFK in Dealey Plaza – to protest that his hardship discharge from the Marines was altered to "undesirable" due to his defection.

Oswald thought that the soon-to-be Governor Connally was still the head of the U.S. Navy at the time he wrote the letter. Was it possible that Connally knew of this Oswald defector? Did Oswald know Connally? Did Connally ever receive that letter?

If so, Oswald possibly presented himself as the perfect patsy, the commie defector-fall guy.

It should be noted that Connally wanted in on the presidential ticket in 1960. Before he was appointed Secretary of the Navy at LBJ's behest, Connally wanted to be on the 1960 Democratic

Presidential ticket. Connally even expressed a disdain for Kennedy, publicly denouncing his ability to be President with his Addison's disease.

Why would Connally resign a higher-paying, Federal cabinet position to run for the governorship of Texas after only 11 months on the job? Could the Bay of Pigs fiasco have played some part in his resignation?

Were plans in place for the assassination of JFK as early as 1961?

In *Me & Lee*, Judyth Vary Baker alluded to the fact that the plot to assassinate Castro in Cuba shifted to JFK in Dallas, with the same operators and plans. The FBI had been compromised due to the fact that Mafia or CIA agents had "dirt" on J. Edgar Hoover – who could have been disgraced and damaged if it were disclosed that he was a closeted homosexual.

I recalled seeing Judyth Vary Baker for the first time on the History Channel's series *The Men Who Killed Kennedy*. Instead of getting Castro, it would prove easier for "The Men Who Killed Kennedy" to get JFK.

Baker told me in a 2013 interview that her "book tour" and rare appearance in New Orleans was just that ... rare. Baker said that she had appeared by Skype to visitors of the bookstore in New Orleans. She said that she "could not get a guarantee from the Governor of Louisiana" that she would not be picked up, or arrested, for appearing in the state.

When I asked why, she claimed that she feared being arrested by people who accused her of having foreknowledge, or plotting with Oswald, in the assassination of JFK.

I again thought of Rose, as I often do.

Here was another woman in Louisiana who possibly had some foreknowledge of the assassination of JFK.

When I am in Eunice, on any typical work day, I often think of Rose as I travel the U.S. Hwy 190. This was the same road that Rose and the possible assassins traveled.

When I first drove into town, back in 2010, I caught myself looking along the side of the highway, looking for the unknown. As if I might spot some clue, some trace of Rose Cherami.

I found the unknown and tried to make it known. The facts that I have brought out about Rose Cherami only lead me to ask more questions.

One day I drove by the old Moosa Hospital in Eunice. I considered going inside the abandoned and boarded-up facility to get some photographs. I was told that the hospital was now a den of homeless, drug-addled vagrants who could be randomly spotted at night urinating off the roof top. The old hospital, for all of its historical significance, has been defaced by weather and vandalism over the years.

Is it appropriate that these vagrants, the tortured souls and ghosts of human beings – who could be seen as "children of Rose Cherami" – now haunt, in life, the place that Rose haunts in death?

I drove around the side of the hospital, near the emergency room entrance, to take photographs of the exterior. I then drove around to the back of the two-story complex where Rose Cherami once stayed, a place depicted in an Oliver Stone film.

It was then that I noticed it. It was so eerily coincidental that I had to take a photograph.

A road ran directly behind the Moosa Hospital, and if it continued the road would run directly into the hospital.

It was Rose Street.

The cross street: Charmaine.

The street signs for Rose and Charmaine Streets forced my hand to take a picture. It was a close enough coincidence, I figured.

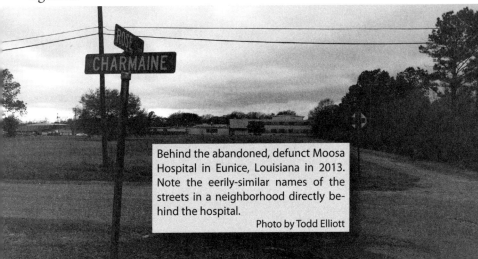

Behind the abandoned, defunct Moosa Hospital in Eunice, Louisiana in 2013. Note the eerily-similar names of the streets in a neighborhood directly behind the hospital.
Photo by Todd Elliott

I wondered to myself, after I took in the still shot, if we as a people would listen the next time another Rose Cherami came along.

In the words of John F. Kennedy, from his final speech given in Fort Worth on the day he died:

"This is a dangerous and uncertain world.... No one expects our lives to be easy – not in this decade, not in this century."

Index

Index

A

Amarillo Globe-Times 75

B

Baker, Judyth Vary 31, 77-78
Bowers, Donn E. 29-32

C

Carousel Club 7, 54-57
Carrier, Jane 14, 45
Carrier, L.G. 14-15, 45
Castro, Fidel 31, 78
Central Intelligence Agency (CIA) 48, 78
Connally, John 77-78
Costello, Frank 35
Crowley Post-Signal 74

D

Davis, John H. 9, 39
DeRouen, F.J. 20-22, 68
Dragna, Jack 56
Dr. *Mary's Monkey* 39-40, 77

E

East Louisiana State Hospital 20-21,
    23, 29, 30-31, 44
Eunice News 13, 21, 28, 67, 74

F

Farewell to Justice, A 24
Federal Bureau of Investigation (FBI)
    5, 14-15, 24-25, 27, 40-42, 44-
    46, 51, 53-54, 58, 78
Ferrie, David 31, 57
Fritz, Will 27
Fruge, Francis vii, 9, 16, 19-20, 23-28,
    31, 40, 42, 51, 67

G

Garrison, Jim 3, 21, 26-27, 53-55, 57-
    58, 66
Griffin, Burt W. 56

H

Haslam, Edward T. 39-40
Holiday Lounge 33, 35
Honolulu Advertiser 77
House Select Committee on Assassi-
    nations (HSCA) vii, 4, 20, 24,
    29-30, 43, 51, 58-59
Hubert, Leon D. Jr. 56

J

JFK (film) 1, 70, 73
Johnson, Lyndon 77-78

K

Kennedy, John Fitzgerald vii, 1-4, 10,
    13-15, 21-30, 32-33, 35, 39-40,
    42-44, 51, 53-54, 57-60, 63, 67,
    70, 73-74, 76-79
Kennedy, Robert 39-40, 74
Kilroy's 9-11
King, Martin Luther Jr. (MLK) 58-59,
    74
Kirkland, Sally 1

L

Legacy of Secrecy 33, 59
Life (magazine) 77
Long, Huey P. 35
Louisiana State Police 5, 19, 24, 27,
    31, 41, 44, 51

M

Mafia Kingfish 9, 39
Mamou Hospital 36
Manuel, Edison 34
Manual, Eugene 33-38

Manual, Mac 27
Manuel, Hatley 10-11, 33-36
Manuel, Linda 33, 35
Marcades, Michael 8, 25, 66-69, 71-72
Marcello, Carlos 9, 26, 31-40, 59
Me & Lee 31, 77-78
Mellen, Joan 24
Men Who Killed Kennedy, The 78
Mills, Chris 19
Milteer, Joseph 59
Moore, Jerry Don 61-65
Moosa Hospital 13-20, 45, 79-80
Morein, Wayne 25, 27-28, 40
Murret, Dutz 31

N

Newsweek 77

O

Odom, Frank 20
Office of Strategic Services (OSS) 48
Oswald, Lee Harvey 4, 10, 15, 25-28, 31, 40, 61, 73, 76-79

P

Pavur, Louis 13-16, 45
Perrin, Robert L. 56-57
Pink Door 26

R

Ray, James Earl 58-59
Rich, Nancy Perrin 55-58
Roosevelt, Franklin D. 48
Roselli, John "Handsome Johnny" 43
Roselli, Sam 37
Ruby, Jack 4, 7, 15, 25-28, 43, 54, 57-58, 61, 63, 73
Rusk, Dean 77

S

Savoy, Bobby 37-38
Savoy, Frank Jr. 36-38

Savoy Hospital 36
Silver Slipper 2, 7, 9-10, 23, 26
Springfield Daily News 76
Stone, Oliver 1, 9, 70, 79
Stroud, Minnie 59

T

Thompson, J.T. 13
Time (magazine) 77
Tippit, J.D. 57, 76
Trafficante, Santos "Sam" 33

V

Vasser, Carina "Sue" 38-39
Vernon, Matt 28

W

Waldron, Lamar 33, 59
Weiss, Victor 29-30